With *Blessingways*, the art of childbirth preparation is entering a new age. For several decades the focus has been on classes for pregnancy. The word "pregnancy" was suggestive of "class..." ... and eloquent way to change the focus and to look back on the primary, universal and forgotten need of pregnant women to feel that they belong to a community of women.

—**Michel Odent, MD**, obstetrician, author of *Birth Reborn*
and founder/director of the Primal Health Research Centre

Blessingways reads like a full blessing in itself. This work embodies the grace of pregnancy through its inspiring and practical wisdom. It is now recommended reading for all students of midwifery at Hygieia College as well as my friendship circle. The ideal gift for any expectant family, *Blessingways* is an excellent resource for celebrating life's happiest, if most ordinary, miracle.

—**Jeannine Parvati Baker**, midwife, author of *Prenatal Yoga &
Natural Childbirth,* and founder of Hygieia College

Pregnant women and their friends will find inspiration in *Blessingways* — a wonderful guide that synthesizes generations of experience with Blessingways. Practical and creative suggestions help anyone tailor the way an individual mother is honored. What a wonderful way to welcome a new life into this world!

—**Rahima Baldwin Dancy**, midwife, author of *Special Delivery* and
You Are Your Child's First Teacher, and founder of Informed Family Life

Blessingways is a soulful resource for families as they await their baby. This nurturing guide is like a warm, welcoming embrace that provides fresh inspiration for an auspicious beginning for the new mother and her baby.

—**Andrea Alban Gosline**, author of *Celebrating Motherhood,* the *Mother's
Nature Calm and Confidence* cards, and *Little Moments of Peace*

Well-written, well-researched, wonderful...*Blessingways: A Guide to Mother-Centered Baby Showers* is an important book for American women to read. The importance of having a Blessingway during pregnancy is to honor the woman and empower the woman. Stronger women are stronger mothers so babies also benefit. Blessingways are relevant to every pregnant and birthing woman, to every family expecting a child, to the relatives, friends and neighbors, to the local community in which the family lives, and to all society. Honoring pregnant women is the way forward to a stronger world.

> —**Marsden Wagner MD, MS**, Former Director of Women's and Children's Health, World Health Organization

Blessingways is a must-have for any woman approaching birth and for those who are supporting her into motherhood. You can pick and choose the rituals which ring true to you from the myriad of possibilities, and easily create a beautiful and empowering ceremony.

> —**Francine Krause**, Pregnant BellyMask pioneer/artist

This magical book made me realize that the baby showers commonly held in American society are more focused on the baby than the mother; the gifts provided at such showers have the utilitarian function of giving the mother a full layette for the baby, but do not provide much space for honoring the woman herself as she makes her life-changing transition into motherhood. In contrast, the Blessingway as Maser describes it is specifically for the woman-becoming-mother, to honor not only her transition but also her entire life and her essential beingness. *Blessingways* is chock-full of examples of specific Blessingways, of how Blessingways can be tailored to the individual woman's particular characteristics and life circumstances, and of mothers' deep and heartfelt appreciation for the acknowledgement and empowerment these woman-designed and woman-centered rituals provide. As I read these enchanting pages, I wished that I myself had been honored as woman and becoming-mother in such extraordinarily empowering ways. And so it is my hope that this book will bring the Blessingway into wider social consciousness, and that every becoming mother might be so celebrated and so blessed.

> —**Robbie Davis-Floyd, PhD**, author of *Birth as an American Rite of Passage*

A must-read, must-do for every pregnant family...*Blessingways* speaks to the sacred nature of the pregnant woman, and allows us to remember the very important and somewhat neglected spiritual elements of birth. If all babies and their families were honored in this way, I believe we would see the evolution of a more nurtured, caring society.
  —**Anna Kealoha**, author of *Songs of the Earth* and *Trust the Children*

This thorough book is a welcome addition to my library, although I guarantee it will not sit on the shelf at all! Kudos and gratitude to Ms. Maser. She has understood and explained the value and the *necessity* of ritual and ceremony as it pertains to the passage of birth, and in doing so, has given birthing women an invaluable "remembering."
  —**Nancy Wainer, CPM**, co-author of *Silent Knife: Cesarean Prevention and Vaginal Birth After Cesarean* and author of *Open Season: A Survival Guide for Natural Childbirth*

This book presents an important ritual to childbearing women of the 22nd century. Shari shows us how to celebrate one of life's greatest rites of passage with courage and an open heart. The women in this book support their community of expectant mothers by sharing their wisdoms, insights, compassion and victories. This knowledge helps the expectant mother to more readily meet birth head-on and fulfill for herself and her family the tremendous potential inherent in birth. I have practiced the ritual of Blessing Way into birth for more than 30 years, and I find that it is one of the best and sweetest lessons for preparing a woman to birth.
  —**Raven Lang**, midwife and Doctor of Oriental Medicine

Blessingways is terrific. It is both timeless and timely. The celebrations are imaginative and different. For those who want to produce a very special event, this book can give them all the creative ideas they need.
  —**Mary Embree**, mother of two

Beautiful! Every pregnant woman and childbirth professional in America should add this gem to her library!
　　　—**Mickey Sperlich, CPM**, midwife

Since the early 1980's, when I was first taught the art and ritual of Blessingway by Jeannine Parvati Baker, I have led, participated in, and experienced Blessingways. Blessingway is a powerful tool for women's empowerment as we approach birth and motherhood. With the potential to ease fear, increase confidence, and surround the mother with the sense of support that has been shown to improve birth outcome for mothers and babies, the Blessingway should be considered an important part of prenatal care. Shari's book has provided a practical and beautiful tribute to Blessingway that will allow anyone interested to create this important celebration for their friends, family, or clients.
　　　—**Aviva Romm, CPM**, midwife, President of American Herbalists Guild and
　　　　　author of *The Natural Pregnancy Book, Naturally Healthy Babies and
　　　　　Children,* and *Natural Health After Birth*

So much more than the traditional baby shower, *Blessingways* celebrates a woman's transformation through pregnancy and childbirth, using ritual to honor this rite of passage and to affirm that in her family and friends she will find the support she needs. Reading this unique book you will find yourself looking for opportunities to share the many variations it describes with the expectant mothers in your life.
　　　—**Marian Tompson**, co-founder of La Leche League International

Shari Maser has woven together invaluable stories from countless women across the country and from many different traditions. In reading *Blessingways*, I felt like I was happily reliving the Blessingways I had attended, and re-experiencing the joy and connection to women through the ages. I can't wait to plan my next one!
　　　—**Merilynne Rush, RN, BSN**, Traditional Midwife and Board of Directors,
　　　　Michigan Midwives Association

Blessingways can have an enormously positive spiritual, emotional, and physical impact on women's childbearing experiences. This dynamic introduction to Blessingways demonstrates how to give such a valuable gift to mothers-to-be.

—**Sierra Hillebrand, CPM**, midwife, doula, and childbirth educator

This unique book details the who, when, where, what, why, and how of mother-centered baby showers. The Blessingway is an intimate event and reading this book can be too as you read how women have celebrated their transition into motherhood. *Blessingways* will help you plan *your* Blessingway so that it is special and extraordinary to you.

—**Paulina (Polly) Perez, RN, MSN, FACCE**, perinatal nurse, and author of *The Nurturing Touch at Birth* and *Special Women: The Role of the Professional Labor Assistant*

An indispensable guidebook for the pregnant or adoptive mother as she celebrates her transition into motherhood. This book is filled with ideas to support and empower women in their quest to honor themselves and each other as they give birth to our future generations.

—**Barbara Brookens-Harvey, MSW, CSW**, prenatal yoga instructor

A baby shower is a wonderful way to welcome a new child. But a Blessingway honors the mother and the many roles she plays. This is a much-needed paradigm shift. With its accessible introduction to the Blessingway concept and its applications in today's world, *Blessingways* will benefit every woman who reads it.

—**Sarah Hamil Bajc**, CEO of Kideapolis and mother of three

BLESSINGWAYS

A Guide to Mother-Centered Baby Showers
Celebrating Pregnancy, Birth, and Motherhood

BY SHARI MASER, CCE

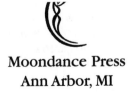

Moondance Press
Ann Arbor, MI

Blessingways: A Guide to Mother-Centered Baby Showers—Celebrating Pregnancy, Birth, and Motherhood

Copyright ©2004 by Shari Maser

ISBN 0-9754551-7-6

First Edition

Printed in the United States of America

Library of Congress Control Number: 2004105849

Book and cover design by Robert Aulicino
Cover illustration by Marci Tarre
Musical transcription by Kristi Bishop
Cover photo from Nan Koehler. Thank you to Shari Garn for being such a beautiful Blessingway momma!

An exhaustive effort has been made to clear all reprint permissions for this book. This process has been complicated; if any required acknowledgements have been omitted, it is unintentional. If notified, the publishers will be pleased to rectify any omission in future editions.

Published by:
Moondance Press
4830 Dawson Drive
Ann Arbor, Michigan 48103 U.S.A.
(734)426-1641
www.blessingway.net

For my daughters Alex and Erica, and for my sister Marci
—May you walk in beauty
—And may you find fulfillment in
sisterhood, womanhood, and motherhood

ACKNOWLEDGEMENTS

Special thanks to...

My mother and father, Judy and Mike Tarre, for teaching me the value of family, and for loving me always.

My sister Marci, for her ongoing support and loving kinship.

My daughters, Alex and Erica, for being my guiding lights.

My husband Steve for his unwavering love through the vicissitudes of life.

Dana Beth Perlman, for showing me how "feminist" and "feminine" can go hand in hand, and for her everlasting friendship.

Barbara Harvey, for teaching me, through example, about grace, courage, equanimity, and the power of positive thinking.

Tina Stone, for her wise counsel and life lessons about faith, love, patience, self-discipline, generosity, and the importance of listening.

My circle of friends for helping to make Blessingways a reality in Ann Arbor, and for giving me the gift of one.

My midwives, Mickey Sperlich, Sierra Hillebrand, Merilynne Rush, Kerry Lizon, Rahima Baldwin Dancy, Valerie El Halta, and Bridget Ciupka for being there in loving service when I needed them.

Karen Ungar, Cathy Daub, and BirthWorks, for helping me get out of my head and into my body and soul — as both a teacher and a birthing woman.

Martha Laatsch, Cathy King, and Inward Bound for inspiring me, through yoga, to live life more mindfully.

Ute Arnhold and Rosalyn Tulip, for giving me such a positive introduction to the womanly arts of birthing, breastfeeding, and mothering.

Wendy Young, for her keen insights about humanity, ceremony, and building interpersonal connections and cross-cultural respect in our diasporic country.

The Ann Arbor District Library staff for their cheerful and untiring support of my research.

All of the wonderful mothers, writers, artists, musicians, and friends who have helped me find my way — Sarah Hamil Bajc, Jeff David, Ellen Bogard, Amanda Smith, Sandra Greenstone, Misti Smith, Kristi Bishop, and countless others.

And my deepest gratitude to...

Jeannine Parvati Baker, Raven Lang, and Nan Koehler for translating the Diné Blessingway tradition into a form that could be applied to contemporary American pregnancy and birth, and for their teachings about this evolving ceremonial concept.

and to...

The Diné people, whose wisdom and traditions inspired their work and mine.

CONTENTS

I.   A BLANKET OF LOVE – 1

What is a Blessingway? — 1
Why Choose a Blessingway? — 3
The Blessingway "Quilt" — A Womanly Art — 7
Three Stories — 7

II.   SELECTING THE PATTERN:
      PLANNING A BLESSINGWAY – 13

The Planning Process — 13
    Who, When, Where, What, Why, and How — 16
    Invitations — 27
    RSVP's — 40
    Creating a Ceremonial Atmosphere — 40
    Preparing for the Ceremony — 43

III. PIECING THE QUILT TOGETHER:
      RITUALS AND CEREMONIES – 47

Ceremonial Progression — 47
Ceremonial Options — 51

Music — 52
    Singing and Chanting — 52
    Bells — 54
    Drumming — 55
    Toning — 57
Evocations — 57
    Invocations —57
    Smudging — 60
    Silence — 61
    Guided Meditations — 62
Grooming the Mother-to-Be — 69
    Footwashing — 73
    Hairbrushing — 74
    Headwreaths —77
    Belly Art — 77
A Sharing Circle — 79
    Naming/Appreciations — 81
    A Blessingway Bracelet — 81
    Candlelighting — 83
    Readings — 86
    Storytelling — 88
    Beads — 90
    Gifts from the Heart — 95
    Wishes for Baby — 101
    Corner Stones — 103
    Birthing Power Shirts — 103
    Releasing Fears — 105
    Belly Masks — 106
    Quilts — 110
    Planting a Tree — 112
    Prayer Showers — 115

Physical Touch and Movement — 116
  Arches — 116
  Cradling — 120
  Circle of Love — 121
  Laying on of Hands —122
  Moon Salutations — 124
  Walkabout — 128
Breaking Bread Together — 128
  Libations — 128
  Blossoming — 130
  Feasts — 131
Reaching Out — 136
  Meal Trains — 136
  Long-Distance Blessingways — 138
  After the Baby is Born — 139
Sample Ceremonies — 143

IV. VARIATIONS ON THE PATTERN: BLESSINGWAYS FOR OTHER TRANSITIONS —153

Adoption — 153
Grieving the Loss of a Baby — 157
Other Occasions — 164

V. SCRAPS AND THREADS — 171

Women Across North America Share Their Insights — 171

Chants, Songs, and Suggested Sources of Music —187
Sample Readings and Suggested Sources of Readings —217

VI. THE FABRIC SHOP – 225

Recommended Reading: More Information About Blessingways — 225
Other Selected Resources for a Holistic Approach to Pregnancy,
     Childbirth, and Parenting — 230

Bibliography — 248

Index — 251

PREFACE

I do not consider myself an "expert" about Blessingways — I am simply a woman who has participated in a number of Blessingways, done extensive research on the subject, interviewed lots of women, and catalogued their ideas, insights, experiences, and collective wisdom to share with others who are interested. In this book, I have not given you all the "right" answers. I have simply passed along what I have learned so far about the possibilities.

I am forever learning more from each and every woman I encounter. Please help by sharing your own Blessingway experiences.

Shari Maser
4830 Dawson Drive
Ann Arbor, Michigan 48103
www.blessingway.net

A BLANKET OF LOVE

What is a Blessingway?

Blessingways are woman-centered celebrations. The emphasis in a Blessingway ceremony is on heralding the expectant mother — her strength, her beauty, her dignity, her womanhood, her divine procreative powers, her metamorphosis as she goes through the creative process of bringing new life into this world.

Baby showers are usually more baby-centered parties that help prepare a layette for the newborn. They first appeared in the United States after World War I and have become widespread since the end of World War II. A baby shower can be a wonderful blessing. It can give the pregnant woman a forum for sharing her excitement about the baby soon to be born. It can bring friends and family together to feast, chat, laugh, and celebrate. It can ease the financial burden of preparing for a new member of the family, and provide the expectant parents with some of the necessities.

The games, gifts, and topics of conversation at baby showers classically focus on the baby and touch only the surface of the pregnancy, birth, and parenting experience. But now, in a return to more traditional ways, many women are also choosing personalized Blessingway ceremonies that focus on celebrating the pregnant woman and her transition through childbirth into motherhood.

Since the 1970's, American midwives — led by Raven Lang, Jeannine Parvati Baker, and Nan Koehler — have loosely adapted these celebrations from the traditional Diné (Navajo) Blessingway, a sacred fertility rite. In addition to the borrowed term Blessingways, women have called their ceremonies Mother Blessings, Birthing Ways, Belly Blessings, and Alternative Baby Showers. To me, Blessingway most aptly expresses the essence of these ceremonies. "Blessing" connotes spirituality and community connections, and "Way" reminds us that every change is a process, an ongoing journey along the path of life.

So Blessingway feels like an appropriate word to use when we honor a woman's transformation through pregnancy and childbirth into motherhood. When using the term Blessingway to describe this evolving ceremonial concept, let us remember to respectfully acknowledge and appreciate its sacred Diné heritage as our source of inspiration.

Contemporary Blessingway ceremonies follow no prescribed rules. They simply provide a forum for those who cherish a woman to express their support through various traditional and non-traditional rituals.

For some women, the Blessingway can take the place of a conventional baby shower. For many women, it makes sense to have both a baby shower and a more intimate Blessingway. Another variation is the combination Blessingway and baby shower, with the usual baby gifts opened after the ceremonial portion of the event, or possibly even sent home for the mother and father to open at a later time.

Blessingway ceremonies can be religious or secular, multicultural or specific to the honoree's heritage, newly created or ancient, simple or elaborate, tightly structured or open to improvisation. The common thread among Blessingways is the use of ritual to celebrate the mother-to-be, to acknowledge the momentous impact of bringing a new baby into her family, and to support her through this transition.

For me, a baby shower is like a McDonald's Happy Meal. It's fun, it fills a need, and you get to keep the gifts afterward. So that's good. But a Blessingway is even better. It's like a romantic date at a five-star restaurant — somehow all the perfect elements are combined so that it nourishes both the body and the soul.
— Emily

There's no booty of pink and blue gifts. The Blessingway is about the woman we know best — not the unknown baby inside her, but our friend and sister, the mother-to-be.
— Sue Robins, from "The Blessingway: An Alternative Baby Shower"

Why Choose a Blessingway?

Women's reasons for choosing Blessingways are many and varied.

For Rhonda, it was the shift from the baby shower's typical emphasis on the baby to the Blessingway's focus on addressing the holistic needs of the pregnant woman herself — tending to her body, mind, heart, and spirit. Isabelle was seeking a symbolic initiation into the circle of mothers. Colette needed to pull together a strong circle of female support, an intimate group of women she could count on to be there for her after her baby was born.

Robin wanted a ceremony that would honor the uniquely female rite of passage through birth into motherhood. Marsha wished to celebrate the magical transformation that occurs in the childbearing year, and prepare for the joys and challenges of birthing and parenting. For Jamie, most important was taking the time to reconnect with her inner self, Mother Nature, and the divine.

Lynne was seeking empowerment, affirmation, and inspiration in preparation for childbirth. Dionne, who was pregnant with her fourth child, looked forward to being celebrated as a lifegiver. Sandy was hoping to bolster her faith in her ability to birth a baby vaginally after having had two previous cesarean births. Jenny was looking for a spiritual way to enrich her experience of pregnancy, birth and parenting. And Mary's goal was for both her and her husband to gain some confidence as they approached the threshold to parenthood together.

Pregnant women tend to be wide open emotionally. They seek spiritual growth, deep personal connections, and opportunities to explore and validate their innermost fears, hopes, dreams, worries, and expectations about bringing a baby into the world. A Blessingway can fulfill those needs by delving into the meaning, the impact, and the universality of a woman's transition from pregnancy through childbirth into motherhood.

In our fast-paced society, it is often difficult to make time to meditate, pray, or consider the changes childbirth will bring to our body, mind, and spirit. Blessingway rituals lead us to slow down, look inward, and embrace the life experiences we are passing through. For an hour or more, the Blessingway gives us an opportunity to focus our attention, within a loving circle of support, on the incredibly joyful and sometimes painful transformational process of pregnancy and birth. It gives us a gentle way to bid a formal goodbye to the old (before-baby) world and welcome the new (with-baby) world in its place. The ceremony can also underscore the sacredness of birth, and remind us of the value of trusting both our own intuitive wisdom and the collective wisdom of women through the ages.

Birth is one of the major rites of passage in a woman's life. A Blessingway acknowledges and celebrates the challenges, pleasures, and spiritual growth inherent in this journey from womanhood to pregnant womanhood to new motherhood and beyond. The rituals of a Blessingway can help ease and define these transitions in a woman's life by demonstrating our love, support, and encouragement; evoking positive images; lovingly addressing her fears; and helping her feel the power of sisterhood. Through the Blessingway experience, she can gain confidence, courage, and equanimity which will carry over into birth and parenting as well.

Most women are surprised by the intensity of emotion and the depth of spiritual awakening they experience during a Blessingway. In this way, the ceremony is similar to labor; in fact, I consider it to be a valuable part of a woman's preparation for labor.

The ceremony gives the mother a chance — on a smaller scale — to yield to her own inner power and the emotional power of having other women fully supporting her; to "go with the flow" of energy created as an experience unfolds; to acknowledge that birth can be mysterious, challenging, unpredictable, magical, intuitive, and sacred; and to feel with all her being the sanctity of life-giving. I can think of no better foundation for birth and parenting!

Like all ceremonies, religious or otherwise, Blessingways can infuse a group with reverence for life and a feeling of communion with nature, the divine, and each other. Their rituals unite women, giving them a potent sense of purposefulness that can engender individual and collective joy, encouragement, inspiration, healing, and empowerment. Thus, Blessingway ceremonies have a positive impact on all of the participants.

> My Blessingway ended up fulfilling its intended purposes and much much more. I was surprised, because I felt shy and nervous initially, and wondered what I was getting myself into. Everyone did. But not for long. It felt too *right*, too perfect to feel awkward. It was like my friends were my cheerleaders, and I was the home team going into the biggest game ever. This was the pep rally, and it pumped me up with love and courage and confidence and readiness. It prepared me psychologically for the challenges and surprises ahead. And it made me feel like a winner.
>
> — Lisa

> We have very, very few opportunities in our lives to feel truly honored, where other people are honoring us not for what we do but for who we are. You might get an award for something you accomplished at work, but that's not the same as being honored for who you are as a person, and the roles that you play — as a mother and a sister and a friend and community member.
>
> — Melisa

The point is to make the transition into motherhood a healthier process. I think postpartum depression often comes from lack of confidence, lack of a support system. But a Blessingway can mobilize a woman's support network and foster confidence.   — Rachel

For my husband and me, the Blessingway was a deeply religious ceremony. It was a way for us to invite God more fully into our hearts and minds, and to reaffirm our trust in Him.   — Lynette

I'm not a religious person. But the Blessingway gave me a chance to affirm my own faith — in myself as a woman, in my body, in my community of friends and family, in Mother Nature.   — Kathleen

My purpose in doing it was to honor my friend and bless her, and to have her feel totally embraced and surrounded by the love of women. I wanted her to feel nurtured and supported as she went into the birth process. I wanted her to feel this sense of solidarity from other women, and to feel empowered and awed by the mystery of what she was going through.   — Bronwen

We're giving Stacy a Blessingway because she's planning a VBAC [Vaginal Birth After a Cesarean]. She already has one kid so she doesn't need more baby things; what she needs is courage, healing, and faith in herself and her body.   — Liz

I remember leaving there thinking that it was one of the most beautiful moments of my life, and that if every child came into such nurturing, loving energy, that it could transform the world!   — Diana

The Blessingway "Quilt" — A Womanly Art

Planning a Blessingway is a lot like making an heirloom quilt — inspired by love and guided by the wisdom of other women, absolutely anyone can do a beautiful job. Just as in quilting, women planning a Blessingway use whatever materials are available or affordable or strike their fancy to craft a deeply personal treasure. Bits of beauty from many sources are bound together into one priceless blanket of love.

As you begin your Blessingway "quilting" process, you may discover that an existing pattern or template looks just perfect to you. If so, by all means use it, and personalize it. But if nothing appeals to you, follow your intuition and design your own. The possibilities are almost limitless.

In planning a Blessingway, just as in quilting, there is no one-and-only pattern, style, or technique. Every quilt is unique, just as every woman is unique, and every pregnancy, every birth, every baby, every family. For that reason, this book does not provide you with a ready-made template for Blessingways; instead, it offers you ideas to inspire your own inner creativity.

Happy quilting!

Three Stories

Angela's Story: Getting Ready

My Blessingway was very simple, but boy, what a punch it packed. My sisters, my mom, and four close friends gathered at my house. My youngest sister Rita had cleaned the house from top to bottom the night before, so all I had to do was be ready. That was a treat!

The ceremony began with Mom brushing and braiding my hair while Rita painted my toenails. We talked about the symbolism — how this was my time to be on the receiving end of the nurturing that I was being called upon to give in such abundance to the babies growing inside me; how changing my hairstyle represented the great transformation of giving birth; how the circle of life connects mother to daughter to unborn children. When I was all styled, Mom presented me with a purple velvet maternity shirt she had worn when she was pregnant with me and then with Rita. I put it on and it made me feel like a mother.

Then everyone spoke about me, and what they appreciated or valued most about me. Even my sister Marianna, who generally keeps her thoughts and feelings to herself, cried and said how important my loyalty had always been to her, and how she thought that would translate into my being an awesome mother. It bowled me over, hearing so many expressions of love all at once. I felt completely affirmed — as a sister, as a friend, as a woman, as a woman about to become a mother.

We had a group hug, then Rita broke out her guitar and some of my friends picked up drums and rattles and they sang to me — songs about birth, about being strong like a mama bear, about being loved and supported by all these other women. I felt really energized.

Finally, Mom called the men to come on over. They showed up with a truckload of food and we had a huge feast, complete with mock champagne for a toast to me and Joe and our growing family. Joe said the guys had been really cool over at Dad's house, telling stories about their own kids and teaching him some lullabies and just generally psyching him up for becoming a daddy.

When we went to sleep that night, we both agreed that we finally felt READY for the babies to come. That day will always be the second-most amazing day of our lives, after the actual day the twins were born!

Kate's Story: An Affirmation of Faith

I had a classic baby shower first. It was great fun — a big crowd of extended family, friends, and coworkers came and we played parlor games and opened presents. So the baby's layette was complete, and I was very thankful.

The next day, my friend Roz orchestrated a Blessingway for me. She invited just my mom, my grandmas, and my most intimate friends to her place, out on her patio. We had a moment of silence, then my Grandma Sarah led everyone in prayer. In addition to the usual prayers, there was a candlelighting ritual. Grandma Sarah lit a votive candle on the table beside me, saying "I pray for courage for Kate and her baby." Each person lit a candle and added something to pray for: joy, equanimity, good health, faith in God, a strong sense of humor, wisdom. With all the candles lit, everyone joined hands to sing "This Little Light of Mine, I'm Gonna Let it Shine."

Roz led us in a tea-sharing ritual. She served hot tea into each person's hand. As we held it and tasted it, we were all symbolically sharing the pain of labor, as well as the pleasure of bringing a baby into the world.

Then we had a feast-time ritual. Roz had asked everyone to bring a dish that had symbolic meaning, and now they took turns explaining what inspired them. My mom brought strawberries and cream, representing fertility and mother's milk. My friend Em had baked a round challah with poppy seeds on top — the seeds of life and the circle of life. Liza cut up two ripe melons that she laughingly compared to my bosoms. Grandma Sarah made deviled eggs; she said that eggs always made her appreciate women's divine procreative powers. And Grandma Lorraine brought wine and fresh-squeezed lemonade for us to celebrate with; she explained that they signified the bittersweetness of labor, motherhood, and life in general. After we had shared a taste of all these special offerings, we sang "I Am As God Created Me" and "As We Bless the Source of Life." And then we feasted!

The ceremony affected me more deeply than I had ever imagined it would. By the end, I felt just like a ripe peach bursting with life-force, ready to drop from my momma tree and send up a baby shoot. My faith in the rightness of God's plan for me was affirmed. So was my confidence that my friends and family would share all the joys and sorrows of my life with me.

Shari's Story: A Personal Growth Experience

Big with child, I feel full and round and luminous like the moon on this silvery winter night. I make my way to Eleanor's side door. She greets me with a warm hug, unburdens me of my coat and boots, and slips my feet into some woolly moccasin slippers. Then she leads me to her guest bathroom, aglow with fragrant candles. I inhale deeply, and exhale out all the cares of the day.

Refreshed, I return to the hallway, where Eleanor gives me a steaming mug of red raspberry leaf tea, then leads me around the corner where a friendship arch awaits, formed by the arms of my dearest friends. As Eleanor purifies the space with burning cedar, I amble through the archway while everyone smilingly sings: "From a woman we were born, into this circle, from a woman we were born, into this world." I feel encircled by my community.

I am ensconced in an antique rocking chair draped with quilts and my mug of tea joins a glass of water, a box of tissues, and a vase filled with sprigs of baby's breath on a small table. My friends settle into their seats in intimate silence. I feel incredibly relaxed, completely open and receptive to the love and support that surrounds me. I rock quietly for a minute or two, relishing this feeling.

Although I am not a religious person, it seems fitting that Eleanor invites the Higher Spirits into the room with this invocation: "We turn to the North, and ask for power and wisdom during Shari's labor. We turn to the East, and ask for Shari to be in touch with the inner knowledge of her body that already knows how to give birth. We turn toward the South, and ask your blessings in this season of Shari's sexual life. We turn toward the West, and ask your guidance and courage in Shari's transformation from mother of one to mother of two."

The archway, the chanting, the invocation have all combined to transform this familiar living room into a sacred space. Somehow, introductions now seem in order, even though we have all known each other for years. Eleanor draws upon my Jewish heritage with a naming ritual, asking each woman in the circle to introduce herself in turn, in this way: "I am Shari, daughter of Judy, daughter of Vivian, daughter of Dora…" We each recite as many generations of mothers as we can remember.

This ritual of naming is a potent reminder of the interconnectedness of all women, from generation to generation, and of the fact that we were all borne by another woman, who was borne by another woman, who was borne by another woman…It feels right to offer a tribute to the women who mothered us, and to recognize our place in the line of mothers before us, thereby honoring the timelessness of the work of pregnancy, birth, and motherhood.

Because I am the one about to embark on the path of motherwork, they now symbolically prepare me for that journey. My childhood friend Christine brushes and styles my hair, drawing out my feminine side. Accepting this nurturing act is good practice for me, since I know birth will soon demand from me this very kind of sensual, womanly strength — yielding, softness, responding viscerally to loving touch.

Meanwhile, my midwife Mickey washes my feet in a bowl of warm rose-scented water, which transports me into a daydream. Two women walk together along a winding path. The younger woman has great strength and is obviously the leader. The older woman is the navigator, a loyal helper who uses her wisdom, skills, and tools to ensure that her friend reaches her destination safely. This vision clarifies the roles that Mickey and I will play in birthing this baby; she will accompany me on the labor path as my guide and protector, but it is I, standing on my own two feet, who will bring forth this baby. The power, the lifeforce, is in me. I accept, in this moment, that this is the way it should be. Mickey dries my feet and gently massages them. They feel reinvigorated, ready to carry me through labor and beyond.

As I am groomed from head to toe for my new role as a mother of two, my friends assure me of their continuing love and support by singing an old folk song: "Dear sister, dear sister, let me tell you how I am feeling. You have given us your treasure. We love you so."

The sharing circle now begins, with everyone honoring me as a woman and a mother. Eleanor adds a red dahlia to the crystal vase of baby's breath on the table beside me. She shares a poem aloud, then she presents me with a goddess pendant for a "birthing power" necklace we will make. She adds four ceramic beads, two large and two small, for the three members of our family plus the one to come.

Each of my friends follows, with a flower, a reading, and a few beads they have chosen. There is a bear, signifying strength, a cowrie shell as a sign of fertility and a wide pelvis; two birds for freedom, a silver African bead symbolizing the universality of birth, and many others. As these gifts from the heart pour in, the tears pour down my cheeks. Finally, I add three polished coral beads my mother gave me long ago, as I shyly give voice to the three affirmations that have encouraged me throughout my pregnancy: "My body is beautiful and strong...I accept the healthy pain of labor, if and when it comes...I share in the strength and wisdom of all mothers."

Photo by Cindy Wauer

This opens the door to a frank expression of my innermost fears about this pregnancy (my second), fears I have been afraid to admit to up until this moment. It is liberating to be able to give them voice, knowing I won't be judged. I realize I have been struggling to say my affirmations; now within this circle of faith and understanding, I am able to embrace and truly believe them.

The circle is closed with the same song with which it was opened, but now it is spontaneously sung in the round. I feel completely nourished and filled, but of course I still have room for Christine's homemade raspberry chocolate cake.

The vase and the necklace come home with me as tangible reminders of the intangible gifts — womanpower, love, encouragement, faith — bestowed upon me by my circle of friends. I carry the positive Blessingway energy with me as I birth Erica.

And today, five-year-old Alex asks, "Mom, will you give me a Blessingway when I have a baby?" "Sure," I beam, "What shall we do at your Blessingway?" "Oh, mom, I don't care what we do. I just want you, Erica, and my friends to be together in that special way that makes our lovehearts grow," she answers sagely. "But I sure do like those bead necklaces..."

II

SELECTING THE PATTERN: PLANNING A BLESSINGWAY

A quilt is an assemblage of fabric swatches organized into a cohesive pattern. Similarly, a Blessingway ceremony consists of many pieces — the people, the rituals, the location — stitched together into one meaningful pattern. Usually, some advance planning and preparation precedes the creation of both quilts and Blessingways.

The remaining chapters of this book will guide you through the process of fabricating your own unique Blessingway ceremony.

The Planning Process

A Blessingway can bring the power of ritual and ceremony into our lives in recognition of the transformational nature of pregnancy, childbirth and parenting. There is no such thing as a standard Blessingway; each ceremony is individualized.

As you plan a Blessingway, you will tailor it to fit the particular woman being honored and blessed. Consider her unique personality, her sense of style, her fears and needs as a pregnant woman and mother-to-be, any wishes she has expressed, and her family, religious, and cultural background.

Her personality will help you determine, for example, whether or not she would be comfortable receiving a footbath, or whether she would feel slighted if conventional gift-giving were omitted. Your use of candles, flowers, music, decorations, and food should suit her personal taste. Do your best to meet her needs, from pampering to empowerment. Weaving her own heritage into the celebration can personalize her Blessingway and imbue it with deeper meaning.

Sometimes Blessingways are impromptu happenings, but most are crafted in advance. Anyone can plan a Blessingway, so if you are a friend or relative who would like to give the gift of ceremony, go ahead and offer to plan one!

Since you will be creating a profoundly personal and spiritual event, you may feel more comfortable sharing the responsibility with one or two others. It can be fun and productive to brainstorm and plan together, and it makes things easier if you can divide up the preparation and hostess duties. Be sure to communicate well and often, though. I have found it helpful to put things in writing as they are agreed upon, so that each person can keep track of the overall plan as well as her own role and responsibilities.

It may be exciting to involve everyone who will attend the Blessingway in the planning process. Planning it in concert with them lets you draw upon all of their energies. "When the community becomes involved in the preparation process, they make the ceremony more meaningful for themselves and the honoree. Energy and attention is given to details and the strength of their love unfolds," explains midwife Nan Koehler. People can be invited to share ideas for the ceremony, or to bring contributions such as music, food, flowers, or prayers.

A Note to Midwives, Obstetricians, Childbirth Educators, Doulas, and Other Practitioners Serving Women in the Childbearing Year:

You may have the opportunity to give the gift of a Blessingway. Some practitioners guide each client's friends and family through planning a Blessingway for her. Others craft simple private ceremonies for each expectant mother and her partner (and children). Still others design seasonal group Blessingways for their clientele.

Many childbirth educators incorporate blessing rituals into their classes, often in the form of a ceremonial send-off. Practitioners sometimes serve as facilitators at clients' Blessingway ceremonies; this dovetails nicely with their role as facilitators during pregnancy and birth.

You too can adapt the ideas in this book to share with your clientele. If you would like further guidance, Blessingway pioneer Jeannine Parvati Baker offers a variety of workshops. Find out more at 435-527-3738, www.birthkeeper.com or www.freestone.org.

Photo from Nan Koehler

The Blessingway should not be a forum for your own beliefs and style, but rather a framework for the pregnant woman to express and share her own spirituality or sense of self. The participants are all there, in a way, as a flattering mirror, to reflect her strengths, ideals, beliefs, personal growth, and beauty back to her. Usually, the best way to facilitate this is to include the mother-to-be in the planning process.

Who, When, Where, What, Why, and How

Once you have committed to planning a Blessingway, you can begin to piece it together. Some questions to consider asking the honoree include: who, when, where, what, why, and how.

Who

Who would you like to invite? Shall the guest list include women only? Women and lap babies? Entire families? Men and women but no children? Please provide a list of guests' names, addresses, and phone numbers and/or e-mail addresses. (Return the guest list to the honoree for easy reference later, e.g. for thank you notes or birth announcements.)

Blessingways are such intimate events that the guest list should be chosen with care. It might make sense to invite only her closest friends and relatives; to choose only those people in whose presence she feels positively about herself; or to select those who share, understand, or are comfortable with her desire to mark this life-change ceremonially.

Because pregnancy and childbirth are uniquely female experiences, Blessingways are usually women-only affairs (with or without lap babies).

Toddlers can definitely be a distraction and men will certainly change the tone of the rituals, but with a little creativity, they too can be included.

Involving children, especially siblings of the coming baby, can be valuable. It gives the children an opportunity to participate actively in honoring the pregnant woman and welcoming the new baby; it introduces children to the concept of motherhood as a spiritual journey; and it can fill girls with a sense of pride about belonging to the universal circle of women.

A Blessingway for both the father and mother acknowledges the shared nature of the transition into parenthood and reaffirms the couple's commitment to raising a family together. "A circle including both men and women will help to draw the father into the aura of support," says Nan Koehler.

Women have found many innovative ways to involve men and children in Blessingways. For example, a Blessingway given on Sandy's birthday began with a women-only ceremony, then turned into a family barbeque immediately afterward. At a family-inclusive Blessingway welcoming the Lechners' newly adopted baby, each man, woman, and child shared a song or reading and lit a celebratory candle (toddlers had help). The hosts of LaTonya's Blessingway invited the men to sit in an outer circle around the inner circle of women and witness, but not participate in, the ceremony; men and women then joined together in celebration afterward. Becki and Rob were both seated in a place of honor at their Blessingway, where they were pampered with massages, bestowed with blue corn necklaces, and offered songs, prayers, and wishes for themselves and their new baby. Amy's sister planned three concurrent events — a Blessingway for Amy and her circle of women in one room, a Blessingway for the father and all the men in another room, and a babysitter for the children in the back-yard. Afterward, everyone gathered together for cake and icecream, along with a song and a candlelighting to give the children a taste of ritual too.

Intergenerational Blessingways can be especially exciting. In addition to children, consider inviting the mother of the pregnant woman, her husband's mother, their grandmothers, and other older women with whom she has a special bond. Including youngsters and elders acknowledges the continuity of the circle of life.

A Note to Men

In this era when there are strong societal pressures for men to play an active role in every aspect of birth, parenting, and housekeeping, it may surprise you that I am encouraging the women in your lives to consider ceremonies that do not include you. However, even though your wives, mothers, sisters, girlfriends, grandmothers, and woman-friends love you and wish to involve you in their lives, it may feel intuitively "right" to them for the Blessingway ceremony to happen in the realm of the female, in the same way that breastfeeding naturally does.

A certain magical feminine energy arises in a women-only circle that can inspire and sustain a woman at a time when she is being drawn deep into the mysteries of womanhood. As the woman prepares to grow and nurture and birth a baby, she can gain great courage, confidence, and comfort from sharing her rite of passage with other women who have done or will do the same.

It is a strong and giving man who can step back graciously and let that happen without him, even if he plans to be an active participant in the birthing of the child.

Of course, for various reasons, some women and men will prefer to join together for a Blessingway, and will find value and power in that approach. See above for suggestions about how to weave men into a Blessingway ceremony.

My husband loved the music, he loved the women that were there and all the prayers, the stories, the laughter. In a way, he needed the support as much as I did — we already had a one, three, and five-year-old so when I have a baby he has to take care of me and take care of all the little kids.
— Sandra

I definitely needed my Blessingway to be a "woman thing." And my husband was so sweet to understand that this was only for me, even though I want him involved in the birth.
— Laurie

An all-women circle will usually have more depth of sharing and intimacy, while a circle including both women and men will help to draw the father into the aura of support. It's helpful to ask men who do attend to come as a "sister" or a friend.
— Nan Koehler, from "Blessingway (California Style)"

We've maintained it as a women's ceremony. Where the men participate is they cook for the women and they bring the food. And they nurture the women in that way.
— Cindy

It seems like an important part to me, that it be a woman-only thing, and women unburdened by other responsibilities. You can't give of yourself fully when you have children around because your first responsibility is to them and you have to respond to their needs.
— Melisa

I had invited the friends whom I had invited to attend my homebirth. I felt like it would be important energetically to create sacred space together in preparation for labor and birth.
— Teri

The children and spouses of my female friends were with me at my Blessingway. The children came with their natural curiosity for ritual and ceremony and celebration.
— Francine

I did invite some women, two that I knew quite well, two that I didn't know very well, and then I invited another woman who was "the white-haired one." I had a very interesting mix of women and it was one of the most amazing experiences of my life. The two women that I didn't know well came with such giving and revealing of themselves, I'm still lifelong friends with them.
— Sandra

A lot of the Birthing Ways we've done also include bringing the pregnant woman's mother and washing her feet, honoring her as well, as the lineage holder for this new child. She would be there because we were honoring the pregnant woman's motherline. The father's mother brings the motherlines from the other direction and represents the fatherlines.
— Gae

I wasn't even going to invite my mom, but my sister suggested it. It ended up being good that I included her. She was a really big part of the day, and we got a lot closer after that. I hadn't even planned on having her in the hospital with me, but then she ended up being right next to me when Isaac was born, holding my hand as I pushed him out. I don't think that could have happened if she hadn't been at the Blessingway. It just would have been awkward, but it wasn't awkward because we'd already reconnected. So the Blessingway was kind of a big turnaround thing, and I'm really glad she was there.
— Stephanie

When

When shall we celebrate your Blessingway? Let's choose a date and time.

Blessingways can be appropriate at just about any time. Most Blessingways occur during the third trimester of pregnancy, when pregnant women are usually most open to — and most in need of — connection with other women, affirmation, and focused attention on the coming birth. A Blessingway often feels intuitively right just before the time of birth; the immediacy of it energizes, encourages, and inspires the mother.

Of course, it is difficult to know what dates will be precisely prior to the baby's birth, since due dates are just estimates which leave you a six- or seven-week range of possible birth dates to plan around.

You may want to follow the matriarchal tradition of scheduling ceremonies at either the full moon or the new moon, or the Native American tradition of performing a Blessingway ceremony when the moon is waxing full. For adopted babies, a Blessingway just before or soon after the family brings the baby home might make sense. For a woman expecting multiples, you might target an early date, since mothers of multiples often give birth weeks before their estimated due date. A Blessingway can be held after the baby is born, too.

Inquire about the honoree's preferences. If she has recurrent nausea in the afternoons, for example, a morning gathering might be in order. If she has always dreamed of having high tea then you could honor her wish and plan a late afternoon event. If her husband or child care provider is only available on Saturday evenings, then that may be the deciding factor.

Your own needs and the needs of the other participants might also affect your selection of a time. For example, if the woman's sister works nights, you might be advised against planning an early morning event; if your lap baby's fussiest time is usually in the early afternoons, you might avoid that part of the day.

When planning an outdoor event, consider environmental factors. You might avoid a summer evening Blessingway in the Michigan woods, for example, because the mosquitoes could interfere with everyone's focus and enjoyment. Also for outdoor gatherings, perhaps a raindate or alternate location should be identified.

A Blessingway ceremony can take an hour or more. It is vital to allow plenty of time for the rituals, so that no one feels rushed. This can be accomplished either by scheduling a generous block of time for the Blessingway gathering, or by leaving the ending time unspecified.

> We met at sunrise in the mountains. We just couldn't pass up the symbolism, as the impending birth was going to be the dawn of motherhood for Elise.
>
> — Gina

> I really wanted to do something special to celebrate Carrie; for her to relax and really focus on herself and this baby; and to remind her that these people love and support her and that she could do it. And I tried to make it as close to her labor as possible so she could carry that with her.
>
> — Karen

Where

Where will we gather together?

There are advantages and disadvantages to every possible location. Let us examine three popular choices: the honoree's home, your own home, or a park. But keep in mind that there are other options as well, such as a religious sanctuary, a private room in a restaurant, or a beach.

One advantage to planning a Blessingway at the honoree's house is that she does not have to go anywhere. This is ideal for women who prefer not to travel, either because of the discomfort of riding in a car when pregnant, or because of specific needs relating to the pregnancy (such as a familiar array of comfort foods that she can access instantly whenever nausea hits, or a chair that fits just right to alleviate the ache in her back).

Many women are also more emotionally at ease at home. It is said that home is where the heart is. For a pregnant woman who is focusing her energies on home and family, it can add power to bring the ceremony into her hallowed homeplace.

Rituals such as Corner Stones (see page 103) can bless the family home. Flowers, candles, and altars can continue to adorn the home long after the Blessingway is over, giving the expectant parents ongoing inspiration, joy, and courage.

A possible disadvantage of bringing the Blessingway to the honoree's home is that she may feel obligated to play the role of host. You can take the pressure off, though, by making a point of arranging to handle all the details — such as cleaning her house; providing all the food; washing the dishes; or adding a ceremonial touch to the space by rearranging the furniture, lighting candles, or setting out vases of flowers. While you prepare her home, draw an herbal bath for her to luxuriate in, or send her out for a massage (or into another room — many massage therapists make house calls).

Hosting the Blessingway at your home may make it easier for you to get everything in order, from cleaning the bathrooms to finding the matches at the last minute. It might also be less intrusive for the honoree.

In your home, you can be certain that she will feel like a guest of honor. However, she may be tired, hungry or sore after a long ride to your house. Or you simply may not have the space available to accommodate the number of people on the guest list.

A park can be a lovely place for a Blessingway, especially since being outdoors underscores the pregnant woman's connection with the earth and all living things. Nature is full of surprises, though, so you will not have control over such unexpected things as snow in late April, goose droppings on the beach, or strong winds. It can also be more difficult to ensure privacy in such a public place. Still, the beauty and power of an outdoor Blessingway may be worth the creative effort necessary to overcome such potential obstacles.

> I had homebirths and I had the Blessingways in my house so they sort of blessed my home.
> — Sandra

I had my first Blessingway in my mother's home, which was perfect — it brought everything full circle. Returning to my childhood home as an adult about to bring my own child into the world really helped me, and my mother, to make peace with this transition. It gave us both a chance to say a final goodbye to my child self and a welcoming hello to myself as a mother.

— Kathleen

As comfortable as the woman might feel in her own home, I never have the Blessingway in her own home...There is too much stuff that goes on with women: Is my home clean enough? Did everything get cleaned up properly? Did all the decorations get taken down? And all kinds of things. So she gets the leftovers, she gets the wreath that we put on her head, she gets all kinds of good things to take home with her, but it's never in her own home.

— Nancy

We like the beach. The ocean holds significance as a symbol of the womb and of the lifegiving force. And I can't think of any better background music than the sound of waves crashing!

— Eve

What

What do you wish to experience or express at your Blessingway? What do you need from us in order to feel supported and affirmed as a pregnant woman, a birthing woman, and a mother? What can we do that will be especially meaningful for you? Is there any ritual or other particular that you feel strongly about having/not having as a part of your Blessingway? Are you comfortable with us planning some surprises or would you like to be fully consulted?

This gives her a chance to convey her specific preferences as well as more general feelings, such as a high or low comfort level with being touched. The "Ceremonial Options" section of this book may serve as a springboard for discussion, as it will give the mother-to-be a sense of the possibilities.

I had the perfect balance between knowing and not knowing what to expect for my Blessingway. My friend who planned it asked me what was most important to me, and she asked me if there was anything I knew I didn't want to happen too. I felt very strongly that some part of the Blessingway should focus on journeys, because the adoption process was really a journey for all of us. So she chose a ritual, a song, and some artwork for the invitation that evoked that theme. I told her that I was open to accepting some pampering on that day, even though that is hard for me, but that I definitely did not want a ritual footwashing, or anything having to do with my feet. So she arranged for me to spend the hour before the ceremony getting a professional massage, then she had a close friend brush and style my hair while everyone sang to me. I was able to express my needs and have them met, yet still maintain some sense of unpredictability and spontaneity. — Barbara

I feel it's essential to ask what she needs and include her in planning her celebration or gathering so it really gives her exactly what she needs. I actually planned two of my own Blessingways. — Lee

Mine was a surprise Blessingway. I probably wouldn't have agreed to one if somebody had offered to plan it for me — I just don't like being the center of attention. When I got to work, I noticed there were extra cars in the parking lot. When I walked up to the front door, the invitation was pinned up on the door. So I walked in and they had all this food out, and they had cleared all the furniture out of one room and made big piles of pillows. The room had flowers all over and they had lit candles. I was totally totally blown away, completely surprised, but happy. — Gabrielle

Why

Why does a Blessingway appeal to you, instead of, or in addition to, a conventional baby shower? What purpose or need will the Blessingway fulfill?

The answer to these questions will give you insight into her hopes and expectations about her Blessingway ceremony. Probing to understand the "why" is key to establishing a clear intent or purpose that will guide you through the rest of your planning.

We asked ourselves, "What is the intention or overall purpose of this Blessingway? What are we really trying to help her with?" We decided we needed to symbolically release her into the world, with her own growing up into womanhood and pregnanthood and motherhood.

— Mickey

I needed as strong as possible a sense of my own capacity and power. I wanted to feel that my own power was connected to that of the other women in my life and to the other women on the earth. I needed to source in some way, that which was bigger than me.   — Stefanie

I very much enjoy a circle of women, and I find that women in a circle raise lots and lots of energy. And I wanted that energy surrounding my child coming to our home, especially because it was an adoption. I thought that it would be very healing and really a welcoming for the baby.

— Barbara

We planned to baptize the baby. But I did not want the miracle of birth and life to go spiritually unmarked until after the baby was born. I wanted to do something special while the baby was growing inside me, to celebrate and venerate the wonders of pregnancy and birth and motherlove.   — Marcy

How

How can we tailor this Blessingway to suit you best? Is there anything you would like to contribute? Please describe your religious or cultural heritage. Is there someone you would like us to consult about your traditions (for example, a family elder or clergyperson)?

Invitations

Invitations are as individual as women. Sometimes telephone or e-mail invitations are most convenient. However, many women prefer to send out written invitations. These can be as simple as a quick written note or as elaborate as a calligraphed card with seashells, a feather, an incense stick, and a crystal attached to symbolize the elements of life — water, air, fire, and earth.

Especially for people who have never encountered a Blessingway before, invitations should be explicit about the spiritual nature of the gathering. They should also specify what, if anything, you expect people to bring (such as a reading, a bead, or a dish to pass). You might indicate how they could be involved in the ceremony too. For example, Kelly's invitation states: "Although everyone will be participating, there are certain roles that need one person to fill. These include: Foot Massage, Toe Nail Painting, Hairbrushing, Headwreath. Please discuss this when RSVPing if you are interested."

Enclosing directions or a map to the location of the Blessingway will make it more convenient for everyone. Participants should also be notified of any backup plans for an outdoor event, such as a raindate or alternate location.

This invitation was sent as an e-mail:

> Please join us Friday at 6:00 as we celebrate Karina's transition to "mother-of-two-hood" with a brief ceremony, singing, dancing, and feasting. Please bring small gifts of sentiment only, and a dish to pass. RSVP to Trish at trishbobish@mac.com
>
>

This invitation was originally shared by Jennifer Louden in *The Pregnant Woman's Comfort Book*:

> You are invited to participate in a baby blessing cermony, hosted by Jennifer and Randi, for Kristina. This ceremony will include singing, meditation, offering Kristina our support, and gifts for her unborn child. The ceremony is relaxing and requires your interaction. We hope you can make it! (Please direct questions to us. Kristina knows nothing!)
>
>
>
> Please bring a symbolic gift that represents a quality or wish you would like to bestow on the baby. For example, you might bring a feather you find to represent the gift of spiritual life. Or a small mirror to represent the gift of being truthful with oneself. The idea is not to spend money, but to represent an intangible wish. Please bring a pillow or beach chair to sit on.

A BLESSINGWAY CELEBRATION

Please join us in honoring
Shari Maser
as a woman, mother and friend.
We will be gathering on
Sunday, July 3 from 10:30am-1pm
at the house of Eleanor Lupinski
777 Forest Avenue,
Columbia

For the ceremony, please bring
• 1-4 beads (we will be
collectively making a necklace for Shari)
• A reading or a song

A late brunch will be served.
We welcome lap babies only, please.
Looking forward to celebrating with you...
Love and Peace...Christine, Louisa & Eleanor
RSVP: Louisa 555-1603

A Blessing Way
for Kathy
Saturday May 20th in Her Home
at 4:00pm

Birth is a very sacred event experienced differently
by each woman who opens herself to its powers.
Come. Gather. Let us celebrate and honor Kathy
as she prepares herself and her home for the birth of
her child. We will begin with a ritual circle
followed by a simple meal.

Please Bring: A token symbolic of your blessing
for the baby (something you've made, found, or
written ~ it will be tied on to a wreath) a candle,
food to share, any musical instrument or song
& any gifts from the heart.

Partners please join Tim at construction site, and all will gather to
share the meal

RSVP ~ Kathi Mulder (231) 929-1563 or Bonnie Marquis (231) 995-0851

You are invited to a Blessingway-Shower
for Marci Rosenberg
who is soon to become an adoptive
MOTHER !!

In addition to the practical side of "showering" her with gifts she and Aaron will need to care for their new little one, we intend to "shower" her with our love and prayers as well, to bless her on her amazing journey to motherhood. So, in addition to your conventional gifts (please call us for suggestions), please bring a small spiritual or symbolic gift to share with Marci — it might be a poem or prayer that is dear to you, a stone, flower, book, song, etc...

Please also let us know if you'd like to bring a dish to pass. Thank you so much for all your offerings!

When: Saturday, May 31st   2-5 p.m.
Where: Lisa Robb's house
213 Arbor Rd.
Rivertown, MI 48111

* map is on the back

Please RSVP to:
Lisa — 313-555-0012 or Leah ~ 313-555-4997

Please join me in giving Rachael a Blessingway to welcome her into the circle of Mothers.

August 12th around sunset, at the river's edge in Delhi Metropark. Bring a dish to pass and a song to share.

R.S.V.P. to Sandra at 555-3568. Thanks!

A Blessing Way
for
Teri Wolf-Kostin

Sunday, July 22, 2001
5:30 p.m.
3516 Old Church Lane, Roswell, Georgia

A Blessingway is a Native American tradition
A time to join together
To bless, offer strength, support and encourage
Teri as she prepares to give birth to her second child

Please bring (or send):
A bead for Teri's birthing necklace
A letter, poem, or verse to share
A frozen dish for Teri's freezer (for after the birth)

Please RSVP
Leslie Sievert @ 770-555-5818

* Casual Attire * Children Welcome *

As a Blessing Way is not a baby shower, traditional gifts for the baby are not expected.
Your gift is your presence and support during this time of growth and transition
in the lives of the Wolf-Kostin family.

The
Blessingway

A Native American ritual
where the women of the tribe
gather in a circle to celebrate
motherhood and women's divine
procreative powers.
    It blesses the way for the child
soon to be born and helps the
mother clear the way and open
to the magic of birth.

The

A necklace will be
strung together with a
bead representing each of
in the circle - to be worn by
Sandra at the birth.

An exchange of simple gifts to
honor and support each other
in motherhood / womanhood.

The Blessingway will be held at
the Lindo Familie's home - the intended
place of birth on:

June 8th at 10:30 a.m.

722 Soule Blvd.
(747-7645)

Heading West on Liberty
turn Left on Soule.
Come to the
end- we're on
the right.

Please call
if you can
not attend.

Ritual

Lighting of candles with prayer
to help greet this passage with
strength and courage - all visualizing a safe birth and a
healthy baby emerging-

Feast, song, poetry,
story . . . -

Please

(1.) A bead.

(2.) A very simple object that you no longer need to offer as a gift to support another woman in womanhood / motherhood.

Bring

(3.) Fruit, cheese, bread or drink to share.

(4.) (optional) Poems, songs, or stories of motherhood and childbirth.

The Circle of Ǧ

Linda Ostrove
Sandra Lindo (with child)
Katherine Katz
Mary Adams
Blanche Price
Linda Wantuk
Esther Centers
Carole Cooke
Mary Lynn Channer
Patricia Bailey
Caite Allum
Carolyn Hejjkal

_____ was born to Sandra, Leo, Nya and Jackson Lindo on:

(date)   (time)

(lbs. oz.)

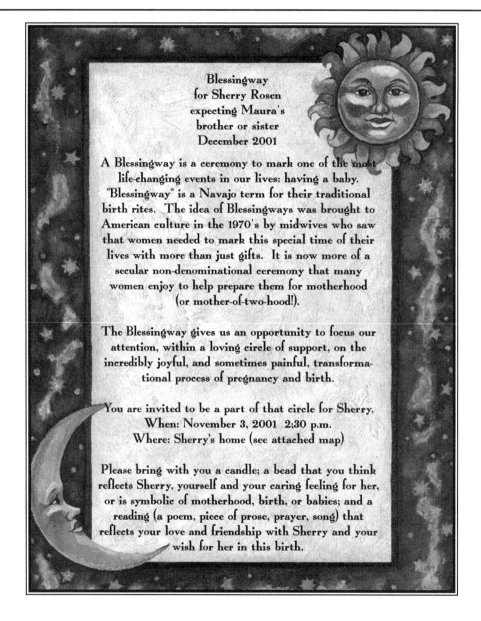

Blessingway
for Sherry Rosen
expecting Maura's
brother or sister
December 2001

A Blessingway is a ceremony to mark one of the most life-changing events in our lives: having a baby. "Blessingway" is a Navajo term for their traditional birth rites. The idea of Blessingways was brought to American culture in the 1970's by midwives who saw that women needed to mark this special time of their lives with more than just gifts. It is now more of a secular non-denominational ceremony that many women enjoy to help prepare them for motherhood (or mother-of-two-hood!).

The Blessingway gives us an opportunity to focus our attention, within a loving circle of support, on the incredibly joyful, and sometimes painful, transformational process of pregnancy and birth.

You are invited to be a part of that circle for Sherry.
When: November 3, 2001 2;30 p.m.
Where: Sherry's home (see attached map)

Please bring with you a candle; a bead that you think reflects Sherry, yourself and your caring feeling for her, or is symbolic of motherhood, birth, or babies; and a reading (a poem, piece of prose, prayer, song) that reflects your love and friendship with Sherry and your wish for her in this birth.

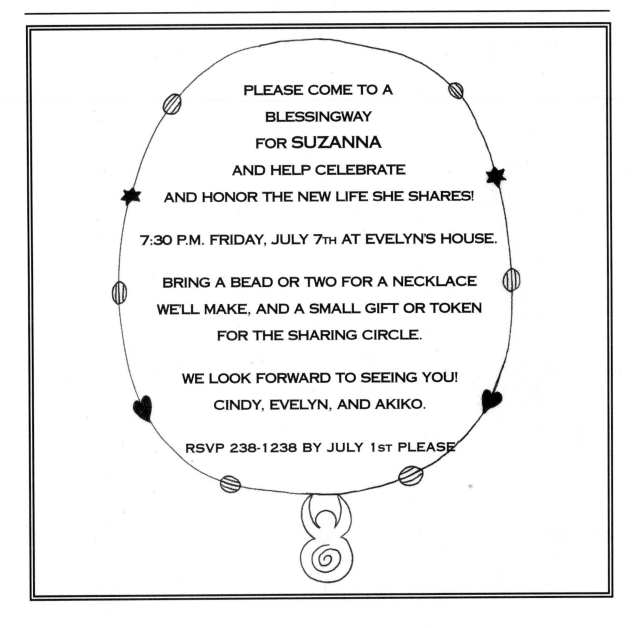

PLEASE COME TO A

BLESSINGWAY

FOR **SUZANNA**

AND HELP CELEBRATE

AND HONOR THE NEW LIFE SHE SHARES!

7:30 P.M. FRIDAY, JULY 7TH AT EVELYN'S HOUSE.

BRING A BEAD OR TWO FOR A NECKLACE

WE'LL MAKE, AND A SMALL GIFT OR TOKEN

FOR THE SHARING CIRCLE.

WE LOOK FORWARD TO SEEING YOU!

CINDY, EVELYN, AND AKIKO.

RSVP 238-1238 BY JULY 1ST PLEASE

This invitation was originally shared in "Blessingway" by Gail Grenier Sweet:

Blessingway for Chris Keller and Child

Blessingway is a ritual which honors the pregnant woman giving birth, heralding her divine procreative powers. It's a special time for us to gather and share our love and blessings for Chris.

March 15th 1:00 p.m. Chris Keller's Home

A time of coming together, relaxing, and getting in touch with ourselves. No hurry. Chanting, singing, quiet talking or waiting silently.

We'll give Chris a foot bath and floral crowning. We'll join in singing "We Are One in the Spirit." Then there will be time to SHARE with Chris your personal wishes, prayers, gift, poem, and so on. Also...we'll present our friendship quilt. After some closing songs and dance and light food, we'll part around 4:00 p.m.

See you!
Ginny

(P.S. Nursing babies welcome.)

Please join me for a Blessing Way & Shower
to honor
Michelle Jones
As we celebrate her pregnancy, birthing and motherhood.

Sunday, September 10th, 2000
1:30 – 4:30
200 10th Street, Brenton, Pennsylvania
Afternoon Tea will be served
R.S.V.P. to Donna Cohen by September 2, 2000
211-555-4567
dcohen@mac.com

or to Michelle by September 7, 2000
211-555-6666
michelle2@mac.com

A blessing way is a short, creative ritual to mark this momentous event in women's lives. It provides a forum to shower love, support and courage on the mother-to-be, surrounded by women who cherish her.

Any of you with specific ideas for the ritual, from the comic to the sublime, should contact Donna. If you have a pregnancy, birth, or early parenting story you would like to share with Michelle, also contact Donna.

RSVP's

When people call to RSVP, you may need to acclimate them to the idea that a Blessingway is more of a ceremony than a party. Give them some gentle guidance, if necessary, about how they can make a positive contribution to the occasion. For example, ask everyone to leave their "war stories" about birth outside the door and share only uplifting stories instead.

Those who are unable to attend the ceremony in person can be encouraged to send a reading, a bead, or some other token so they can still be present in spirit.

Creating a Ceremonial Atmosphere

What is a ceremonial atmosphere? It is a space infused with beauty and reverence. It is a time for focused attention. It is an atmosphere of unity, love, trust, and openness. It is an environment of physical and emotional safety. It is a sense of freedom from the pressures of time constraints and from any awareness of the passage of time. A ceremonial atmosphere activates all five senses, plus the "sixth sense" of intuition and responsiveness to the feelings and needs of others.

It takes deliberate attention to detail to create a ceremonial atmosphere. Whether a Blessingway is religious or secular, it is important to intentionally set it apart from everyday routine. This dedication of time and place fosters extraordinarily moving experiences, and gives people the opportunity to forge deeper connections with their inner selves, each other, their ancestors, and a Higher Power.

In order to create an atmosphere of reverence, the physical Blessingway space needs to be prepared. The participants may also ready themselves for ceremony, both individually — by donning special clothes, meditating, or praying — and collectively — by establishing a shared intention and focusing positive energy in that direction. You can begin to transform any place — indoors or out — into a ceremonial space by adding such things as candles, flowers, beautiful cloth, or a ceremonial display of symbolic items such as seeds or eggs to represent the fertility of the womb.

"There are some specific decorations that are traditionally used to represent the various stages of the birth process," according to Cindy Parker, author of "The Blessingway." "Fresh flowers placed about not only add color and fragrance, but also symbolize sweet conception and the promise of fruit to come. A shell is symbolic of pregnancy itself. It is a water home that nurtures life and protects from outside influences. A hollow gourd reminds us that we are a vessel of transformation, softening through the process of birth. An open seed pod is representative of birth itself, releasing the child and afterbirth."

Pay special attention to preparing the entrance. For example, the entryway could have ceremonial appointments such as lit aromatic candles, a vase of flowers, a welcoming banner, a trellis, or specially selected music playing in the background. These extra touches will help everyone get into the spirit of the Blessingway from the moment they walk across the threshold.

Most Blessingways are performed with all of the participants seated in a circle. For many reasons, circles are ideal: the circle is representative of the natural cycle of life (of which pregnancy and birth are an integral part); the circle is reminiscent of symbols of love such as hugs and wedding rings; the circle is a visual representation of a strongly interconnected community; the circle is a shape that connotes feminine power and beauty; and the circle promotes a feeling of equality, as no one is ever in front or behind. As Nan Koehler said, "the circle is a metaphor for all life, for our planet, for our family circle, for the universe!"

Within the circle, comfortable seating is essential. As an alternative to chairs, each woman may be asked to bring her own throw pillow to sit on. A special seat can be designated for the mother-to-be; traditionally her seat would be higher than everyone else's. In some traditions, the expectant mother is seated above seed corn, representing fertility, growth, and change. A comfortable rocker with a footstool, a luxurious pile of pillows, or a colorful blanket spread over her chair can emphasize her out-of-the-ordinary role as the recipient of extra pampering and attention. In addition to being attractive, the seat of honor should meet the comfort needs of a pregnant woman.

Pregnant women need to drink plenty and often, so be sure to set out a cold drink or a mug of hot tea next to the seat of honor. It is also wise to have handkerchiefs or tissues within easy reach, for those who may need them if the ceremony gets emotionally intense.

Pregnancy Tea

This tea is especially nourishing during pregnancy and postpartum as it contains a wealth of vitamins and minerals, strengthens the uterus, and offers numerous other health benefits. In addition to serving it at her Blessingway, consider bestowing the expectant mother with a supply of tea leaves for the final weeks of her pregnancy and the early weeks of breastfeeding.

Ingredients: Red raspberry leaves and nettles (available in health food stores, or by mail order through Blessed Herbs at 800-489-HERB). You can also add honey, lemon, juice or other herbs such as spearmint to make a more appealing flavor combination.

Directions: Combine one-third cup of each herb in a one-quart mason jar or other airtight, non-aluminum container with a tight-fitting lid. Fill the jar with almost-boiling water and cap it tightly. Let it steep for a minimum of 30 minutes. Strain before drinking. It can be served either hot or iced.

Finally, consider making a checklist of last-minute preparations, such as turning the telephone ringer off, heating water for an herbal footbath, lighting candles, or brewing tea.

Preparing the space is a very important element. The tender care taken to set the mood is just as important to ritual as foreplay is to sex. A wise student of oriental thought once described it to me this way. Man is fire and woman is water. They may come together quickly, creating steam, or the fire may bring the water to gentle boil, with longer lasting effects! I've always remembered that analogy! Anyway, create a pleasant space — peaceful and beautiful, yet powerful.

— Cindy Parker, from "The Blessingway"

We don't decorate the room ahead of time. We transform the room when she's in it. — Nancy

Preparing for the Ceremony

In addition to readying the ceremonial space, it is helpful to do some advance planning of the ceremony itself, and familiarize yourself with each piece of it. In this way, you can ensure that on the day of the Blessingway, the positive energy flow is not interrupted by your own uncertainty or by unanticipated questions of detail. Printing a program can formalize your plans so that everyone can help keep the ceremony flowing smoothly.

For a group that is largely unfamiliar with Blessingways, I encourage you to gather everyone thirty minutes before the honoree's arrival, so that you can communicate more details about the ceremony. You may use that time for some or all of the following:

- Introductions and chatting so everyone can get to know new people and catch up with old acquaintances.
- A brief explanation of what a Blessingway is and why you are joining together for one today. This is also a good time to help people with different belief

systems feel more comfortable with what they are about to experience. Here is an example of a short and sweet explanation offered by Carine Fabius in *Celebrating with Ceremony*:

> "Welcome everyone. The ceremony we are about to partake in has been conceived with love, and it is assumed that all who are here have come to bring wishes of love and well-being to _____ (name of mother or mother and father) and to Baby. The stringing together of certain rituals performed with special intent is called ceremony. Ceremonies are important because they serve to gather up all of our energies and to focus them on one specific thing; in this case, the welcoming (and/or safe delivery of) Baby _____. (baby's name) and to celebrate _____ (mother's name) as she embarks on her new journey as a mother. Choosing a pre-determined time, place and setting for an event; using symbolic words, aromas, sounds, and actions with the participation of special people has the effect of lifting us out of our everyday frame of reference into the realm of the extraordinary, where anything and everything is possible simply because we wish it to be. Though some of the things we do today may seem unusual, know that it has all been carefully researched in the hopes of recreating centuries-old multicultural practices that serve to harness the positive power of the saints, spirits, angels, gods and goddesses that surround us and to make our will known to them..."

⚜ A reminder to leave negativity and scary birth stories outside the door, and to focus only on giving love and strength to the honoree and her baby.

⚜ An explanation of the purpose and meaning behind each ritual. This will help the participants contribute to the ceremony with fuller understanding.

 ⚭ Discussion about the essential role of symbolism in a Blessingway ceremony. Symbolic images, actions, words, and objects have the power to influence people's beliefs on a subconscious level. For example, as Holly Blue Hawkins reminds us in *The Heart of the Circle*, the well-known symbols of a wedding ceremony — the veil, the processional with its evocative music, the kiss, the ring — create an enormous impact. Similarly, a Blessingway ceremony can incorporate symbols such as candles, a string of beads, the binding together of the group with a ball of yarn, or the sharing of special feast foods to signify a rite of passage. Such symbolism adds a whole new layer of meaning and permanence to the experience; the presence of witnesses further increases its impact. The memory of these shared symbolic actions, and the keepsakes that evoke them, will continue to empower the pregnant woman long after the Blessingway ceremony is over.

 ⚭ A verbal run-through and/or a rehearsal, emphasizing special points to remember about "who does what when and where." Here, you may request that everyone stay within the circle (if possible) once the ceremony has begun, in order to avoid interrupting the concentration and energy flow of the group. In addition, you can reassure the participants that there will be time for each of them to share their good wishes and present any offerings they have brought for the mother. If you plan to begin the ceremony with a welcoming ritual such as an Arch, you can also get into position before the mother walks through the door.

 ⚭ An introduction to the lyrics and music for any chants or songs you will sing together, and an opportunity to practice. Songsheets may be helpful for easy reference.

 ⚭ An invitation to follow their intuition and do what comes naturally during the ceremony. Explain that a Blessingway is not rigid in design; that you have only outlined the ceremony, and are counting on each of them to help fill in the blanks through their own inspiration. Similarly, you may want to explain that although you have accepted the role of "facilitator," you are not "in charge"; this is another way of encouraging people to see this as a participatory event. Many people equate the words "ritual" and "ceremony" with inflexibility and a strict hierarchical leadership structure, so it is important to clarify these points.

⚘ Guidelines about when it will and will not be appropriate to take pictures. It is generally wise to disallow videotaping, in order to protect the intimacy of the occasion and the privacy of the honoree. An effective way to limit photography is to designate one person as "official photographer" for the occasion.

⚘ A moment of silent meditation or prayer.

Even within a structured format, there is always room for spontaneity. With flexibility and humor, you can welcome the unexpected. For example, at one local Blessingway, the group decided to forego the last ritual when they became immersed in an impromptu sharing of old family photo albums and reminiscences by the honoree's grandmothers.

That kind of flexibility is invaluable for the pregnant woman to practice before labor, when the unexpected is to be expected. Remember that the Blessingway is being done for her sake, not for the sake of ritual itself, so you can all feel free to let go of the original plan in favor of what comes naturally.

You will find that each Blessingway has its own creative energy. As Connie Banack says in "Blessing Way Ceremonies: A Celebration": "Since Blessing Ways are part of the creative process which is birth — anything can happen." It should be a pleasure for you, with all the planning and preparations complete, to let loose and see how it all unfolds.

III

PIECING THE QUILT TOGETHER: RITUALS AND CEREMONIES

I am often asked the difference between ritual and ceremony. I like to think of a ritual as a swatch of fabric, and a ceremony as a quilt made up of multiple ritual swatches. Which rituals are included and how they all get pieced together varies. This is why each Blessingway ceremony is as unique as any homemade quilt.

The following chapters offer an in-depth look at specific rituals and some ideas for how they might fit together into a ceremony.

Ceremonial Progression

Just as there are many ways to uphold the teachings of most religions, there are also an almost infinite number of ways to give a Blessingway. The form does not take precedence over the content. In a Blessingway, it is the purposeful suffusion with love and attention that is more important than the particular structure.

Early non-Navajo Blessingways generally began with smudging and an invocation. This was followed by singing and chanting; attentions to the mother such as foot-washing and hairbrushing; and a sister-circle that included such rituals as Gifts From the Heart, Readings, and Candlelighting. More singing and chanting and a feast generally brought the ceremonies to a close. Other elements have been introduced as more women have personalized their ceremonies with intuition, knowledge of various cultural traditions, and creativity.

Although there are endless variations possible in terms of sequence and combinations of Blessingway rituals, I encourage you to use this basic ceremonial format: begin with a gentle lead-in; follow it with a period of intense activity, intimacy, and spiritual transformation; then close with joyous celebration. A Blessingway that follows this ceremonial progression will mimic the natural flow of labor.

As you plan, remember that a Blessingway is meant to nourish, not impress. A simple ceremony can be just as fulfilling as an elaborate one. It is unnecessary, and unadvisable, to carefully plot out every detail. Instead, outline a ceremony that leaves plenty of space for everyone to express themselves freely, spontaneously, and without hurry. You will be awed by the unpredictable and synchronistic ways that love will show itself!

> Ritual leaves flexibility for something to bubble up from within, allows space for spirit to enter the picture.
> — Eve

> We try to have a plan, but also leave lots of extra room for the unplanned. Whenever we're together, an energy flows through the group and things just happen. Whatever was planned ends up being different because of the way we approach it that day.
> — Donna

I had debated about the sequence of the afternoon. I decided to do the ceremony, the most formal part, first, and then do the more classic baby shower things afterward, like having lunch and opening gifts. That really worked out well, except that I had a set of expectations for a two-hour event and it ended up being a four-hour afternoon. So three or four people had to leave before the gifts were opened, which was fine, because it felt like it wasn't about the gifts. I think it was more about the connection and the sharing and the support.

— Bobbi

I like Blessingways to have lots of silences and spaces and allow magic to take place, rather than first course, second course, third course, dessert, now let's clear the table.

— Raven

The Beginning

When people arrive for a Blessingway ceremony, they bring a diversity of energy and emotion. A roomful of people, especially those who are not well-acquainted with one another, tends to have an aura of nervous excitement. Therefore, most people choose to begin with calming and centering rituals to break the tension and bring the scattered energy of the group into focus. These rituals create a sense of ceremonial time and space, help everyone feel relaxed and open, and assure the mother that she is safely encircled by those who love her.

Additionally, beginning rituals may provide opportunities for purification or cleansing, declarations of the shared intention or purpose of the gathering, and recognition or appreciation of a Higher Power. Or a Blessingway may begin with a vigil, a waiting for something to happen or for the spirit to move someone to action.

Some rituals that can accomplish the above goals include:

- ⚜ Singing and Chanting (see page 52)
- ⚜ Bells (see page 54)
- ⚜ Drumming (see page 55)
- ⚜ Toning (see page 57)
- ⚜ Invocation or Prayer (see page 57)
- ⚜ Smudging (see page 60)

⚜ Silence (see page 61)
⚜ Guided Meditations (see page 62)
⚜ Naming/Appreciations (see page 79)

⚜ Arches (see page 116)
⚜ Feasts (see page 131)

Holding hands and sharing a few moments of silent meditation can also help establish a mood of reverence.

The Middle

The main body of the Blessingway ceremony generally provides a variety of opportunities for everyone present to shower the honoree with love, support, and blessings. Symbolism is often a key component of this central portion of the ceremony. Grooming rituals may be included to open the mother physically and psychically to accepting nurturing and attention. This can also be an opportunity for her to release and address her fears within the safety of the circle.

Some rituals that can accomplish these goals include:

⚜ Singing and Chanting (see page 52)
⚜ Footwashing (see page 69)
⚜ Hairbrushing (see page 73)
⚜ Headwreaths (see page 74)
⚜ Belly Art (see page 77)
⚜ A Blessingway Bracelet (see page 81)
⚜ Candlelighting (see page 83)
⚜ Readings (see page 86)
⚜ Storytelling (see page 88)
⚜ Beads (see page 90)
⚜ Gifts from the Heart (see page 95)
⚜ Wishes for Baby (see page 101)
⚜ Corner Stones (see page 103)

⚜ Birthing Power Shirts (see page 103)
⚜ Releasing Fears (see page 105)
⚜ Belly Masks (see page 106)
⚜ Quilts (see page 110)
⚜ Planting a Tree (see page 112)
⚜ Cradling (see page 120)
⚜ Circle of Love (see page 121)
⚜ Laying on of Hands (see page 122)
⚜ Moon Salutations (see page 124)
⚜ Walkabout (see page 128)
⚜ Libations (see page 128)
⚜ Blossoming (see page 130)

The End

The conclusion to a Blessingway ceremony can diffuse intensely focused energy and add a joyful sense of closure. Ending rituals help everyone wind down and disengage from the ceremony, while affirming that the blessings or experiences of that day will be carried into the future.

Some rituals that can accomplish these goals include:

- Singing and Chanting (see page 52)
- Bells (see page 54)
- Drumming (see page 55)
- Closing Prayer, Meditation
  or Invocation (see page 57)
- Silence (see page 61)
- Guided Meditations (see page 62)
- Cutting the Blessingway
  Bracelet (see page 81)
- Planting a Tree (see page 112)
- Arches (see page 116)
- Laying on of Hands (see page 122)
- Walkabout (see page 128)
- Libations (see page 128)
- Blossoming (see page 130)
- Feasts (see page 131)

Or, finish as many women's circles do: by raising your arms in sync to send out the energy you raised, stating aloud where you want to direct that energy, then touching the Earth to replenish your energy and ground yourselves.

Singing or saying "merry met, and merry part, and merry meet again" is another time-honored way to close a circle. Dancing together or sharing a group hug can also provide closure. You can then move on to less emotionally charged celebratory activities such as cutting the cake or opening more traditional shower gifts.

Ceremonial Options

This is a "how-they" book — a collection of women's wisdom, experiences and creative ideas that I hope will be both informational and inspirational. What follows are detailed descriptions of rituals from Blessingways all across the United States and Canada. These are possibilities, not prescriptions, so feel free to use them as described here, adapt them, or invent your own!

Music

Singing and Chanting

As anyone who has participated in a campfire circle or religious service knows, singing together stimulates instantaneous unity among strangers and friends alike. Joyful electricity is generated whenever folks join voices in song; it does not matter whether their singing is impromptu or rehearsed, perfectly in tune or simply belted out with alacrity, accompanied by instrumental music or a capella.

In our culture, though, crooning publicly can be far removed from daily life, so some people may not readily sing at a Blessingway. There are many gentle approaches to including tentative singers in singalongs. Playing a recording of selected songs and chants can introduce the choral element into the ceremony, leaving participants free to join in or refrain as the spirit moves them. Strumming a guitar, beating a drum, playing the melody on piano, or starting to sing or chant solo can overcome people's inhibitions about singing. In order to facilitate active participation, it is helpful to either provide songsheets or post the words on a large sheet of newsprint on the wall. Or, keep it simple with a one-word intonation such as Om, Alleluia, or Kyrie Eleison. Making instruments — such as drums, rattles, tambourines, and bells — accessible during singalong times can give non-singers another way to join in the music-making. Even if no one sings, background music is an option.

An opening song or chant helps to focus everyone's energy and attention on the here and now of the Blessingway. Many Blessingways begin with the topical chant, "From a woman we were born into this circle, from a woman we were born into this world." In "Ma Parker's Song Booklet," Cindy Parker suggests singing, "Hello, (name), celebrate (name), sing it with an open heart" to welcome each person attending. Look for more options in Chants, Songs, and Suggested Sources of Music (page 187).

Chants and songs can serve to segue between rituals, to punctuate each person's contribution to a ritual, or to close a Blessingway ceremony. Singing itself can also be the basis for one of the rituals in the sharing circle. For example, invite each woman to share a favorite lullaby, perhaps one sung to her by her own mother.

If you plan a lullaby singalong, you may also ask everyone's permission to record their lullabies for the baby. For women who are timid about singing aloud, this often helps loosen their inhibitions as they feel they are singing directly to the baby, who is a non-judgmental being. On the other hand, recording has the opposite effect on some women, repressing self-expression. So ask for the input of the Blessingway participants, pay close attention to their words and their body language, then make an informed decision about recording their lullabies.

Throughout a Blessingway, dance can be woven into musical moments. Dance adds a more physical dimension to the bond created by singing together. Dancing can be impromptu and simple, or planned and choreographed. Either way, there is intense power in simultaneously reaching up to the heavens with our voices and down to the earth with our feet. It is at once an energy-raising and a grounding experience.

Photo by Therese Langan

I feel united with these women and all women who ever walked the earth. I feel pride; I feel power. And I believe our song pours power into Chris's body, giving her strength to bring forth her babe that grows ready to enter our world.

— Gail Grenier Sweet, from "Blessingway"

Singing and chanting raises power and adds magic. I especially loved the fact that Shauntel made up one of the songs. I think that's a real gift if you can make up a song or chant because that comes from inside you.

— Barbara

I had an impromptu Blessingway. On my last day at yoga class, they all circled around me, holding hands. Cathy put a hand on my belly. Then they chanted "om" five or six times, directly to me and my baby. It seems like so little, but it meant so much!

— Kathi

Bells

It seems that all cultures use music in some way — often as a means of creative expression, meditation, healing, or establishing the bond of spiritual harmony within a group.

Becky Spice, a Wisconsin BirthWorks educator, shares the following insight: "For centuries and in many cultures, bells have been associated with the divine. Japanese Zen gongs open and close meditation, Himalayan singing bowls and tingsha bells are used in Buddhism to purify the mind and create focus. A bell's clear, pure sound is symbolic of creative power and its shape is a symbol of feminine force. [When I first experienced the ritual use of bells,] I could actually feel the vibration of the sound waves as they passed over my body…The purity of tone [in the tingsha bells] is amazing and the duration of the resonance is spectacular. The bells emit a long, haunting echo that has a very calming, soothing effect….They certainly create a sacred space, so it seemed natural to me to bring them into the birthing environment.

"I have found that a sense of ritual helps many women to ride the waves of labor, and ringing the bells with contractions is a beautiful way to do this. The sound will often hang in the air for the duration of a contraction, helping the woman to focus. A lovely bonus, especially in a hectic hospital environment, is the calming, silencing effect it has on everyone present. I have found that the sound commands such respect from nurses, visitors and doctors alike, reminding everyone of the sacredness of the event…Everyone loves the beautiful clear sound which hangs in the air for what seems like forever."

Bells set a joyous and sacred tone. They encourage respectful silence and focused energy. And they keep the pace ceremonially slow.

Ringing a bell or gong can help bring everyone into harmony before the ceremony begins. The ringing of bells can also punctuate each person's turn during a ritual such as candlelighting, or indicate the beginning and/or end of a particular ritual.

If you are unable to find resonating bells locally, they can be purchased through internet providers such as FourGates.com. Or, a rattle, a drum, a shaker, chimes, a chant, or a song can serve as a replacement.

Drumming

Like bells, drums resonate deep within every one of us, evoking the heartbeat and the primitive mammalian self. For a woman about to give birth, it can be especially empowering to reconnect with her animal nature — the raw strength and sleek beauty of a tigress, the physical prowess and fierce loyalty of a mother wolf, the unwavering tenderness of a mama dolphin…

Drumbeats represent the infinite rhythm and pulse of life which fills, surrounds, and connects every one of us at all times. Perhaps because they speak a language with which humans are intimately familiar, drums are very effective at relaxing people and bringing out their uninhibited wild sides. This freeing effect also facilitates bonding within a group, as it inspires increased expressiveness and receptiveness. Drumming is also "an efficient, non-verbal way to synchronize our energies," says Holly Blue Hawkins in *The Heart of the Circle*. "When two hearts are in close proximity to one another they tend to entrain, to find a common rhythm, to 'beat as one.'"

Drums can be used in much the same way as bells: to mark the beginning or end of the ceremony, to create segues, or to punctuate particular elements. Or, drumming can reconnect the circle and raise energy after a hiatus such as a bathroom break. Drums can also accompany songs and chants.

To signify the transition into ceremonial space and time, drums can be beaten rhythmically, carrying everyone into the Blessingway circle one by one. Or, an arch can be formed as a gateway to the circle, with two people standing on either side, each holding a drum, tambourine, rattle, bell, shaker, or smudge stick. Each gatekeeper can shake her instrument or wave the smudge stick all around each woman as she enters the circle, showering her with sound and/or smoke. Finally, the gatekeepers can shower each other, or someone else can shower both of them. If hand drums or other instruments are waiting at each seat, people can join in as they sit down, bringing the music to a crescendo.

Hand drums are wonderful participatory instruments. To evoke the sound of one heartbeat growing into a community of heartbeats, give each person a hand drum. (Perhaps the pregnant mother could be given two drums — a big one and a little one!) A designated leader can start beating a pulsing rhythm, then invite everyone to join in one at a time, either randomly or in order around the circle. "When everybody is drumming in unison, it expresses the eternal rhythm of life, the heartbeat that connects us all, and the joy of life that makes us want to dance and celebrate," observes drummer Lori Fithian.

Call and response drumming is another fun way for a group to bond. One person can play a rhythm (da-da-da-dum) or a pulse (hitting every beat or every other beat), then the pregnant mother and/or everyone else can echo it. Lori Fithian likes to end by saying, "Let that drumming go with you in your journey. Whenever you feel a need to be connected, remember the power of the rhythm, listen to your own heartbeat and take a deep breath."

We use drumrolls after each person's birth story, to say, "we really heard that and took it in and appreciated it."
— Ellen

Do a celebratory jam at the end of the Blessingway — just let go and drum it up!
— Lori

Toning

Like ringing bells and drumming, vocal toning is an effective way to unify the energy of a group.

Toning is usually performed using a Tibetan metal singing bowl (available online through sources such as FourGates.com). A crystal singing bowl will also work, or try toning a capella.

To begin, use the bowl to find a pitch with your voice that feels right viscerally. Hold that pitch, making an open-ended sound such as "aaaaaaaaaah." The other people in the room can chime in one by one as they are ready, matching their pitch to yours. At some point, everyone will "lock in" with such a perfect match that you cannot separate one voice from another. The feeling at that moment will probably be quite electric, yet at the same time the toning will ground everyone by focusing your collective energy.

Toning is sure to have an incredible impact on your group dynamics, as well as on each individual in the group — especially the mother-to-be, as pregnant women are particularly receptive to sensory connections with other women. For this reason, some midwives and doulas use similar techniques to harness the power of voice-matching when working with a woman in labor.

Evocations

Invocations

An invocation draws the beneficent energy of a higher power into the Blessingway space, and focuses the group on the sacredness of the occasion. As Susanna Napierala says in *Water Birth*, invocations may be addressed "to whatever god, goddess, or spirit the mother wishes to honor through her thanks, as well as to ask for strength and wisdom."

The Navajo traditionally do not ask for anything in prayer, but instead surrender themselves into harmony with Nature. Many other Native Americans, when they pray, simply give thanks for the blessings that abound already in their lives. The Judeo-Christian prayer tradition is to express complete acceptance of God's will. Such prayers, devoid of supplication, help prepare the mother to meet the uncertainties of birth and parenting with strength, confidence, faith, and equanimity.

Invocations, prayers, or meditations may open and close the Blessingway ceremony, or be part of a ritual such as Libations (see page 128).

Here are some examples of invocations that may be used in a Blessingway:

   ⚑ From the Christian tradition:
      "God, Giver of Life, Creator of the Universe, we submit ourselves
      to you, knowing all you do is for our greater good. Thy will be
      done."

   ⚑ My friend Melisa gave the following invocation at my Blessingway:
      "We turn to the North, and ask for power and wisdom during
      Shari's labor. We turn to the East, and ask for Shari to be in touch
      with the inner knowledge of her body that already knows how to
      give birth. We turn toward the South, and ask your blessings in
      this season of Shari's sexual life. We turn toward the West, and ask
      your guidance and courage in Shari's transformation from mother
      of one to mother of two."

      One person can lead this invocation, or four kindred individuals can be designated ahead of time to represent the four directions. Each designee can be seated in the part of the circle corresponding to the direction she represents, and then each can recite her portion of the invocation, perhaps adding her own words, a poem, a song, a dance or a gift.

Nan Koehler suggests preparing to call upon each of the four directions by first beating drums, shaking a rattle, or clapping hands four times, then lighting a colored candle representing each direction.

Sometimes more than four directions are called upon. Some traditions, including the Native Americans of the Great Lakes regions, believe that there are seven sacred directions: north, south, east, west, above, below, and within. Speak from the heart as you invoke each of the seven directions.

   In *Casting the Circle*, Diane Stein offers the following invocation:
"We are here to honor (name) who will be a mother. As she makes the passage through pregnancy and labor, she becomes the Mother Goddess and her life will change forever. No more the Maiden, and mature as a lover, she takes on the care of another life with her own. We are here today to invoke the Goddess in wishing (name) a safe birth, a strong child, and happiness in motherhood."

   The following closing invocation was suggested by Nan Koehler:
"We give thanks for the opportunity to gather together in a meaningful way. We give thanks for the form of the Blessingway and for all the loving preparation that went into the creation of this ceremony. We give thanks for the opportunity to honor (the pregnant woman) for accepting the challenge of parenthood. And we remember the sacredness of birth. We thank the Great Spirit and the four directions for helping us and bearing witness to our journey, and we acknowledge the transition of (the pregnant woman) who is now prepared for her new role as mother."

Silence is another powerful tool for focusing the spiritual energy of a group. Include a silent meditation either before, after or in lieu of an invocation. Consider weaving reverential silences throughout the rest of the Blessingway as well.

Smudging

Smudging is a time-honored way of purifying or cleansing an individual or a space. In many cultures, burning sacred plants is thought to ward off evil spirits and protect those brushed by the smoke. Smudging need not be a religious act; it can simply signify your group's intent to create a safe space full of positive energy for the Blessingway.

The Anishnabe Indians and other indigenous peoples of North America traditionally burn blends of dried herbs when they pray, including such plants as tobacco, cedar, and sweetgrass. I encourage you to create your own customized blend instead of trying to recreate the sacred practice of native peoples; for example, one local midwife likes to burn dried roses.

If you plan to smudge, prepare or buy a bundle of your chosen herbs, place it in an abalone shell or a bowl, and light it like incense. Then pass the shell around the circle so each person can wave the cleansing smoke over herself, using either a hand or a feather. Alternatively, the mistress of ceremonies can carry the smudge bowl (or an incense stick) around the circle, smudging each person in turn.

Or, follow a more detailed ritual such as this one described in "Creating a Blessing Way Ceremony" by Robin Sale: "Hold it before you, and center yourself with a calming breath or two. Then draw it towards you with one hand. Bring the bowl to your eyes asking that you may have clear vision, to your mouth that your words may be true and do no harm, draw it to your heart that there may be good sharing, place one hand and then the other above the bowl so that the smoke — the 'breath of the great spirit' — may encircle it to bless all that you do with your hands, and finally let the smoke bless your feet that you walk in a sacred way. Pass the bowl on to the next person."

In *Celebrating with Ceremony*, Carine Fabius recommends that when burning herbs, you "make sure to keep a window or two open so that the smoke and any residue of negative energy may have a point of exit."

Instead of smudging, midwife Cindy Parker anoints each person with flower water as they enter the circle. Bells and rattles are also sometimes used in place of smudging, especially if someone is sensitive to smoke.

Silence

Silence is powerful. It is amazing how quickly and effectively silence brings peace and focus to a roomful of people. Even a quiet minute or two can be calming and centering. Silence is often as richly textured and deeply resonant as music and dance, whether it is a formal, ritual silence or just the reverential hush that naturally fills the air during ceremonies.

Yet for many women — especially those of us who prize being articulate, social, and active in our daily lives — silence is unfamiliar, awkward, and even challenging. It takes effort to still the mind, the voice, and the body and allow a tranquil quietness to envelope us.

It may be helpful to guide your group into silence together. Gently talk them through focusing their breathing and settling their bodies, for example, by saying something like this:

> "I invite you to find a space to sit comfortably...You might want to wiggle your fingers, settle your bottom, stretch your legs, roll your shoulders back and down...Make whatever adjustments your body needs you to make in order to feel perfectly at ease...Now together let's take a few deep breaths. Close your eyes if you wish...Just breathe in and out...in and out...slowly and deeply. Inhale the oxygen, and exhale the stresses of the day...Take a minute to just listen to your breath...Notice the breath of the woman to your left...and the woman to your right...Notice the breathing of everyone around you here...Let yourself be present, here, in this room..."

Wait a minute or two before breaking the silence by humming, singing, or intoning quietly. The others will naturally open their eyes and join in whenever they feel ready. Alternatively, invite everyone to sit quietly, either closing their eyes or looking directly at the pregnant mother, and visualize the birth experience or particular qualities they wish for her to have. Or simply propose a minute of silent prayer or meditation.

In order to establish a ceremonial pace, I encourage you to weave silences throughout the Blessingway ceremony. This will allow quiet time for individuals and the group to process what is happening, absorb the impact, act upon their impulses when the spirit moves them, and bond with one another.

> A time of sitting in silence, perhaps holding hands, just feeling the quietness and the connection with each other — that just gives the sense right from the beginning that it's going to be a ceremony as opposed to a time to just bring gifts and eat.   — Kathi

Guided Meditations

Shared experience creates powerful bonds. A guided meditation creates shared experience by taking everyone's psyche on the same journey at the same time. Thus, it promotes a sense of community, mutual understanding, and togetherness of intent.

Here are two of my favorite guided meditations for Blessingways:

Hand Meditation
From *Celtic Meditations* by Edward J. Farrell. Published by Dimension Books, Inc. Adaptations (in italics) were made by a local midwife.

(To be read slowly and meditatively) *I'd like to invite you all to sit comfortably, and gently close your eyes. Rest your hands open in your lap, palms up...Tune into your breathing...Relax any tension points — your shoulders, your neck, your eyelids, your jaw...Release anywhere you need to...Take three deep breaths, and feel yourself going into your deep center.*

And now become aware of the air at your fingertips, between your fingers, on the palm of your hand. Experience the fullness, strength, and maturity of your hands. Think of your hands, think of the most unforgettable hands you have known — the hands of your father, your mother, your grandparents. Remember the oldest hands that have rested in your hands. Think of the hands of a newborn child, your nephew, *your niece, or your own child* — of the incredible beauty, perfection, delicacy in the hands of a child. Once upon a time your hands were the same size.

Think of all that your hands have done since then. Almost all that you have learned has been through your hands — turning yourself over, crawling and creeping, walking and balancing yourself, learning to hold something for the first time, feeding yourself, washing and bathing, dressing yourself. At one time your greatest accomplishment was tying your shoes.

Think of all the learning your hands have done and how many activities they have mastered, the things they have made. Remember the day you could write your name.

Our hands were not just for ourselves but for others. How often they were given to help another. Remember all the kinds of work they have done, the tiredness and aching they have known, the cold and the heat, the soreness and the bruises. Remember the tears they have wiped away, our own or another's, the blood they have bled, the healing they have experienced. How much hurt, anger, and even violence they have expressed, and how much gentleness, tenderness, and love they have given.

How often they have been folded in prayer, *patience, and meditation*; a sign both of their powerlessness and their power. Our *foremothers* guided these hands in the great symbolic language of our hands — the striking of our breast, the handshake, the wave of the hand in "hello" or "goodbye."

There is a mystery which we discover in the hand of a woman...that we love. There are the hands *of a mother, a sister, a wisewoman, an artist, a healer, a strong woman, a woman in need*. Hands which you can never forget.

*Place your hands on your abdomen, where your womb is or has been. Feel the power there. Honor the depth, the life, the connections to our mothers, the cycles, the rhythm, and the strength. Slowly raise your right hand...*and gently place it over your heart. Press more firmly until your hand picks up the beat of your heart, that most mysterious of all human sounds, one's own heartbeat, a rhythm learned in the womb from the heartbeat of one's own mother. Press more firmly for a moment and then release your hand and hold it just a fraction from your *chest.* Experience the warmth between your hand and your heart. Now lower your hand to your lap very carefully as if it were carrying your heart. For it does, when you extend your hand to another, it's not just bone and skin, it is your heart. *In your handshake or hug you are sharing your heart.*

Place your hands again in your lap. Think of all the hands that have left their imprint on you. Fingerprints and handprints and heartprints that can never be erased. The hand has its own memory. Think of all the places that people carry your handprints and all the people who bear your heartprint. They are indelible and will last forever.

Now without opening your eyes, extend your hands on either side and find another hand. Don't simply hold it but explore it and sense the history and mystery of this hand. Let your hand speak to it and let it listen to the other. Try to express your gratitude for this hand stretched out to you in the dark and then bring your hand back again to your lap. Experience the presence of that hand lingering upon your hand. The afterglow will fade but the print is there forever.

Whose hand was that? *It could have been any hand; it was the hand of a special person. Through our hands we reach each other, help each other, and bless each other. Our hands are essential for the work that must be done.*

The Journey
from pp. 226-229, *The Pregnant Woman's Comfort Book* by Jennifer Louden.
Copyright © 1995 by Jennifer Louden. Reprinted by permission of HarperCollins
Publishers Inc.

We are here today to honor the wondrous event, the incredible transformation, that our friend _____ is in the process of creating. Let's begin by everyone closing her eyes and taking a few deep breaths. (Pause.) Coming into your center, allowing yourself to be calm. There is no place else to be but here, nothing else to be doing but honoring our friend. (Pause; remember to breathe and relax yourself too.) Imagine a circle of light, any color you choose, encircling the group. (Pause.) Now, imagine all the colors intertwining and encircling us in a gorgeous, protective rainbow. (Pause.)

To help _____ remember that she deserves self-nurturing and attention, especially after the baby is born, we will each take turns brushing her hair. _____, allow yourself to relax and take in the attention.

Is there anything you would like to share with us about your pregnancy or your feelings about birth? Specifically, how can we help you in the coming months? (This is a chance for the honored woman to read a letter to her unborn child, perhaps part of the journal she might have been keeping, and to ask for specific help for the coming months.)

Going around the circle, let us each pledge one act of support for after the birth, something specific we can do.

Now it is time for the meditation, for the journey to meet your ancestors. _____, lie down

This is a journey into the imagination for all of us. Together, we will create the energy necessary to take _____ back into the ancient mysteries. Let us all take a moment, again, to close our eyes and sink down, down into our centers, as we are all about to start on a remarkable, powerful journey. (Pause; relax and feel the energy of the room.

If it feels too tense or scattered, turn up the volume of the music and keep encouraging everyone to breathe for two or three minutes.)

_____, breathing in, breathing out, following your breath deep within you, settling into your core of inner wisdom. You are perfectly safe within our circle of light, within this circle of women who love, respect, and want to nurture you. Allow the floor to fully support you. Allow any tension to flow out of your body. You don't need to do anything, you don't need to control this, just let go. Open up and receive. (Speak slowly. Pause often. Sense how relaxed she is and encourage her to let go more if necessary.)

Traveling back through time and space, following your breath back, back to a time when the mystery and power of birth was revered. (Take your time.)

When you are ready, you find yourself standing at the mouth of a cave, with a torch in your hand. Somehow, you know it is the cave that the women in your tribe use for all the mysteries of being a woman: first menstruation, preparing for birth, menopause. (Describe what the opening of the cave looks like to you. Let your imagination speak.) Take a moment to take this in, let it become real to you. (Pause.)

If you are willing and want to, taking your torch with you, climb into the cave. You have to crawl into a damp and narrow space as you enter. As you do, the memory of coming here for your first-blood ritual returns to you. You remember being led here by your mother, your sister, your aunt, and taught the power of being a woman. It feels utterly safe and familiar, yet exciting, as you continue deeper into the cave. (Continue to guide your friend into the cave, explaining as you go what it looks like. You might describe cave paintings you see on the walls, gems gleaming in the torchlight, whatever feels right.)

Dimly, you begin to hear the sound of chanting and drumming. (Indicate to the group to begin singing and drumming softly.) You walk toward the sound. (Pause; let the song go for several rounds.)

In time, you find yourself emerging into a large cavern, lit by many torches. The cavern is filled with the women who have come before you. (Describe women your friend might like to see: her mother, grandmother, aunts, the women present, native women of the land you live on, ancestors unknown but imagined. Tailor the description to her life history.) These women welcome you with their song. They beckon to you. The wisdom, the power, the beauty in this room nourishes you, astonishes you, moves you, sending energy and strength throughout your body. (Pause.)

These women are all here tonight to honor and bless you, to help you prepare for your birth. Tenderly, they bathe you with consecrated herbal water, a gift from the Earth. (Here each woman bathes the hands and face of the pregnant woman while repeating an affirmation.) Some possible affirmations:

There goes all fear you hold about giving birth. The birth will be perfect.

There goes all fear you hold about healing. You will heal beautifully.

There goes all fear you hold about not being a good mother. You will be enough.

There goes all fear of never being creative again. You can have a life of your own.

There go the deepest, most private fears you have about giving birth. You will be enough.

The light from the wisdom and experience of these women streams out of their hands to bless you. (In unison, repeat firmly: "You will be enough. You are strong enough." Here each woman takes turns laying her hands on the pregnant woman, silently imagining healing, loving energy streaming from her hands into the honored woman's body. Take lots of time here.)

The power of all women is with you. (Here is the place to add your own touch: What special help or blessing does your friend need? What elements of her own spiritual beliefs could be incorporated now? Past additions have included reading a prayer, anointing the pregnant woman with cornmeal, talking about a past miscarriage, and a group massage.)

You know the energy and blessing your friends have given you will protect you, will nourish you, through the coming months, through the birth. You know that you only have to remember this, and you will find the strength, the honesty, the courage you need. (In unison, repeat firmly: "You will be enough. You are strong enough." Indicate for the women to start singing the song softly again.) Make any farewells you wish, and when you are ready, you take your torch, and, knowing the wisdom, the strength, the power, and the conviction are always with you, you walk back out. (Describe a little bit of what she saw coming on the journey into the cave but, obviously, in reverse order.) Coming back up, slowly, remembering the blessings, bringing the energy, knowing it is always available to you.

When you are ready, come back to this room (name the town or person's house you are in), back to the circle, ready for our gifts and blessings for [you and] your baby.

A guided meditation can be as simple as this one suggested by Cindy Parker in "The Blessingway": "Everyone holds hands, visualizing the mother in labor, greeting this passage with strength and courage, seeing the baby emerge, and feeling the joy that this new life brings...[After a closing phrase] everyone is then returned to reality as the sacred space dissipates."

You will probably want to customize the meditation you have selected, then practice it so you are comfortable guiding the group on the day of the Blessingway. Or, you may choose a prerecorded meditation such as Layne Redmond's *Being in Rhythm* (Interworld Music, 800-698-6705). Recordings can be beautiful and powerful, although they do not allow for the same kind of personalization as a loving and thoughtful reading (and adaptation) of a text by someone who cares about you.

Be sure to set the stage for your guided meditation. First, make sure everyone is physically comfortable. You may dim the lights, offer pillows for support or blankets for warmth, do a group stretch, or just give everyone time to work out their own bodies' kinks. Then, use music, silence, or words to give everyone the opportunity to quiet their minds and bodies so they can focus on experiencing the meditation within the circle of women present.

When the meditation is finished, give everyone time and space to integrate the experience before you move on to something else. Then, provide closure by ringing a bell, shaking a rattle, beating a drum, singing or chanting, or asking everyone to cherish a few moments of silence together.

Guided meditations can also be offered to the pregnant woman privately, in the minutes or days before or after her Blessingway. To help her open to the Blessingway experience, you might offer a meditation that will let her tune into her own body and its connectedness to the world around her, such as the *Being in Rhythm* meditation or the meditations offered in *Motherhood as a Spiritual Practice* by Patti Sinclair. A meditation after the Blessingway might focus directly on birth, like those offered in *Pregnancy as Healing* by Gayle Peterson and Lewis Mehl.

Grooming the Mother-To-Be

Footwashing

Footwashing is a time-honored tradition in many cultures, from Mayan to Christian. The footbath provides an opportunity for the mother-to-be to practice relaxing into the hands of another and openly accepting the kind of nurturing that she will need during labor. It is also a form of cleansing in preparation for the journey into motherhood. And as a woman approaches the threshold into birth, footwashing can bless her feet and the path they will tread.

A footbath may be performed by the pregnant woman's midwife; the symbolic gesture of footwashing is a tangible reminder of the midwife's role in service to the birthing mother. Throughout pregnancy, birth and the postpartum period, the midwife is part of the mother's support system — giving her love, discerning and tending to her needs, and affirming her body's feminine strength and beauty.

In place of a midwife, anyone close to the pregnant mother can perform the foot-bath — her mother, her sister, her doula, her husband, a dear friend, or the youngest or oldest woman present. It is a loving, touching way for any one of those people to demonstrate a willingness to serve her and care for her as she brings a new life into this world.

Photo from Stephanie Peltier

Before the Blessingway begins, supplies (such as a comfortable footstool covered with a towel, massage oil, or moisture cream) should be set out near her seat for easy access. I recommend partially filling a large bowl with hot water before the Blessingway begins, then adding enough heated water to warm it up again when it is time for the footwashing ritual to begin.

Herbs or herbal extracts such as lavender can be added, and perhaps flower petals could be floated in the water. Either the person who will wash the mother's feet can add all the herbs herself, or each person present can drop in a handful of herbs. Wash and caress the pregnant woman's feet at a leisurely pace. You may then rub her feet with earthy blue cornmeal to dry, soften, and ground them. Then massage them until they feel supple and relaxed.

Meanwhile, a simple song, chant or round can be sung. Or, use this time to share uplifting birth stories; perhaps the mother-to-be's mother can tell the story of her birth, and others can share their birth experiences as well. You may also explain the traditional or personal significance of the herbs, water, and cornmeal as they are used.

Alternatives or additions to footwashing can include handwashing, massaging the mother's feet with aromatic oil, or painting her toenails.

Photo by Mickey Sperlich

Sample Footbath Recipes

Please note that the skin is the largest organ in the body, and anything with which it comes into contact can enter through the pores directly into the bloodstream. So if you wish to add alternate ingredients to a footbath for a pregnant woman, please choose your herbs or essential oils with care; it is advisable to consult a knowledgeable source. Most of the herbs recommended below should be available in any health foods grocery. They can also be ordered in bulk from the Blessed Herbs catalog (800-489-HERB).

Floral Footbath

To warm water, add one or more of the following:

- 2 drops of essential oil of lavender. The midwife or doula can then offer lavender baths and/or lavender compresses when she is in labor; this reminiscence of the Blessingway will bring positive energy into her labor space.

⚶ 2 drops of rose oil. According to Robin Sale in "Creating a Blessing Way Ceremony," this "adds fragrance and a silky texture, and is said to reduce swelling."

⚶ Rose petals floated in the water

Cooling Footbath

To cool water, add:

1 - 2 drops of essential oil of peppermint, which is an energizing and cooling herb. Peppermint makes the skin tingly, thereby evincing a sense of joyous anticipation.

Melisa's Herbal Blend Footbath

Combine any or all of the following symbolic herbs:

⚶ Lavender — for cleansing and purification; symbolizes spiritual sensitivity, remembrance, loyalty, and love

⚶ Mint — promotes health, mindfulness and clarity

⚶ Yarrow — brings inner radiance, strength of aura

⚶ Grape — to encourage trust and positive experience of goodwill from others

⚶ Honeysuckle — for being in the present moment

⚶ Rose petals — represent love, courage, and inner peace and tranquility even in the face of challenges

⚶ Red raspberry leaf— strengthens the uterus

⚶ Comfrey — for healing

⚶ Geranium — for transformation, opening yourself to new levels of creativity

⚶ Bay leaf — for strength

⚶ Marjoram — (just smells nice!)

⚶ Thyme — for courage

- ⚜ Rosemary — for faith
- ⚜ Chamomile — for patience and tranquility
- ⚜ Squaw vine — for strength

Robin Sale points out that even the water itself has significance, as it "represents the blessings of the water element from which all life is born."

For Drying:
Blue (or yellow) cornmeal — Susanna Napierala explains in *Water Birth* that in the Native American sacred tradition, blue cornmeal "represents the source of life and nourishment from Mother Earth. So, drying the mother's feet with the corn meal represents giving the mother the best we have. It also helps her to draw in the nourishment and strength that she needs." Blue cornmeal is thought to bring luck and prosperity, the gifts of the earth element.

Hairbrushing

Birth calls for a very sensual, womanly kind of strength — yielding, softness, responding viscerally to loving touch. For the mother-to-be, letting someone brush her hair can be an opportunity to practice all of that. Hairbrushing also reminds her that she is worthy of being nurtured and pampered, even as she is preparing to nurture a new life herself.

The honoree's mother or another mother figure may brush and style her hair, perhaps while someone else washes and massages her feet. Or, each person in attendance can take a turn brushing her hair.

Letting someone "do" her hair is a positive way to draw out the mother-to-be's feminine side and let her feel especially womanly for a few hours. Changing her hairdo can also be symbolic of the transformation of giving birth. Braids can evoke the image

Photo from Stephanie Peltier

of ripening ears of corn; undoing braids or buns can symbolize opening the passageway for an easy birth. Some say a woman's hair represents her own history, so combing and braiding can symbolize sorting out and making peace with her past. Flowers woven or pinned into her hair can signify the beauty of new life and the flower-like opening of the cervix during labor.

For hairbrushing, set up the seat of honor in a location and position that allows space for someone behind her, and lay out a basket of supplies — a hair-brush, barrettes, ribbons, beads, flowers, vitalizing hair oils (such as lavender), or a head tingler (available online through www.chinaberry.com). You could also include a handheld fan for cooling her if it is a hot day.

Additional ways to pamper the mother and give her a special look on the occasion of her Blessingway include facials, facepainting, manicures, and head-wreaths.

Headwreaths

A floral or ivy headwreath can be the perfect adornment for the mother-to-be. A wreath is reminiscent of a halo (in tribute to the sacred nature of birthing and motherhood) or a crown (symbolic of honor, grace, power and strength, and of being the one whose needs everyone else strives to meet). The circle symbolizes friendship, love, community, birth, and the cycle of life. The ivy and flowers remind us that pregnancy and birth are a part of nature's intricate design.

Crafting an attractive garland does not require any particular skill or previous experience. Try one of the following methods of wreathmaking:

⚘ **Needle and thread:** Choose small flowers or buds with thick bases, such as mini-carnations or sweetheart roses. (A lot of flowers are needed, so for affordability, you might use whatever is in bloom in your own garden.) Use a needle and a doubled, knotted thread to string them together by passing the needle through the center of each flower's head. Sprigs of waxflowers or baby's breath can be added too, by wrapping the thread around the stem a few times, then going back and tying a knot between the sprig and the previous flower. Knot the ends together securely when you have finished. If your thread runs out before the wreath is large enough, do not despair! Just knot the end, then start a new thread by passing it through the last flower on the strand.

⚘ **Florists' wire:** Use florist's wire and corsage tape (both readily available from any florist) to string together small flowers. First, twist a couple of florist's wires together and wrap the connection point firmly with corsage tape. Next, poke one end of the wire through the head of each flower, then secure a bit of stem with corsage tape before adding the next. For sprigs of flowers such as baby's breath, wrap the wire around the stem a couple of times, then secure it with corsage tape.

⚘ **Hot-glue gun:** Use a hot-glue gun to secure flowers to a headband. Or, attach the buds and sprigs to a cloth-covered headband with corsage tape reinforced with scotch tape. (Upon close examination, this will look more amateur, but from even a couple of inches away you cannot tell the difference.) This method is quick and easy, and requires just a small handful of flowers.

⚘ **Weaving with ivy:** Just about any kind of ivy will do, including myrtle and other groundcovers that grow abundantly in suburban backyards. To make an ivy headwreath, first circle a long strand of ivy a couple of times around your own head, leaving a tail of several inches at each end. Then weave the tails into the circle until the ivy holds itself in place. Finally, additional strands can be woven in for a fuller look. Flowers can be inserted easily; perhaps you might ask each woman to add one flower when the mother-to-be is crowned.

Many women prefer fresh flowers and greens because they have life-energy and fragrance. Others prefer no-nonsense silk imitations.

Wreaths with live flowers will look freshest if prepared less than twenty-four hours before the Blessingway and stored in a cooler or refrigerator without any fruit inside. To preserve a headwreath after a Blessingway, simply hang it to dry.

There are many ways to ceremonially crown an honoree. Often, songs are sung to her while her hair is brushed and styled, and then the wreath placed on her head. A few heartfelt words may be spoken about the meaning of the headwreath as it is bestowed upon her. Or, as Cindy Parker describes in "The Blessingway": "The wreath is placed on the mother's head, and she is handed a mirror saying, 'Behold, thou art Goddess...'"

If you do not have the time or inclination to make a headwreath, you might instead supply one flower per person — or ask everyone to bring a flower — to be added ceremonially to a vase of baby's breath or greens. A handmade or beautifully decorated vase will add an extra special touch. The mother-to-be can bring the vase of flowers home to enjoy after the Blessingway ends, perhaps even during labor or after the birth.

> She brought the wreath of flowers and put it on my head, so I felt like royalty or something. It was true honoring. — Kathi

> This vase that everybody had put a flower into, I remember having it in the room when I was laboring and thinking how nice it was to have that presence. — Melanie

Belly Art

Decorating the pregnant belly can be liberating for the mother-to-be and fun for everyone. If your artwork lasts long enough, the belly art can also give the mother a focal point during labor.

Henna ink has been used historically in many cultures to ritually prepare women's bodies for rites of passage. In addition to its artistic value, henna ink has a distinctively cooling effect on the human body; thus, henna on the palms of the hands and the soles of the feet can help a pregnant woman stay cool during labor.

Henna can be used to paint simple or intricate designs onto the body, either free-hand or with a template. Henna art is not permanent, but it will last a number of weeks, so it is worthwhile to practice ahead of time to ensure that you will truly be able to give the expectant mother the gift of a beautiful belly.

Henna supplies may be available in tattoo or henna parlors, art supply stores, and New Age stores. Since there are many do's and don'ts and essential supplies needed for the proper preparation and application of henna, you might prefer the convenience of a kit such as the lovely Earth Henna body painting kit from Lakaye Mehndi Studio (800-224-5600; www.earthhenna.com).

Applying henna is a slow process; during this time, you can use songs, chants, or background music to sanctify the ritual and help the group stay focused.

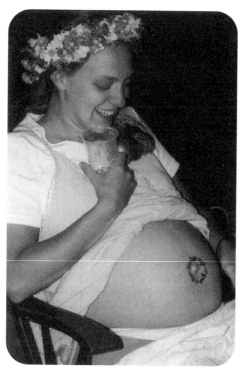

Photo by Mickey Sperlich

Decal tattoos are an easier and less time-consuming option. They are widely available, from Hop-In's to toy stores. For under two dollars, I have seen a lovely ring of flowers that fits just perfectly around the popped-out bellybutton of a pregnant woman.

My friend Susanna received a surprise belly-button tattoo in a suburban backyard, in full view of the neighbors. She was wearing a long dress and thong underwear! Susanna's friends knew her well enough to know that this semi-public disrobing would fall within her comfort zone, but for another woman, it could have been embarrassing or unthinkable. So if you plan to do belly art at a Blessingway, consider forewarning the honoree to dress in a way that provides easy access to her belly while protecting her modesty.

Everyone was invited to paint Marilynn's wonderful round belly. They had so much fun doing this that they spontaneously turned to each other and began to paint one another's faces. In the process of the ritual, a child was lovingly welcomed with intimate prayers and blessings, and a tribe was born!

— Jill E. Hopkins, from *Welcoming the Soul of a Child*

A Sharing Circle

Naming/Appreciations

For people who have never met before, personal introductions are an important first step toward eliminating the awkwardness of unfamiliarity and eliciting the amiable ease of commonality. Even for a close-knit group, there is great value in taking the time to recognize and appreciate each person as an individual link in the chain of loving kinship and friendship.

The ritual of Naming focuses attention on each person's female identity by invoking the memory of grandmothers, great-grandmothers, and so on. Each woman in the circle can introduce herself in turn, in this way: "I am Dana, daughter of Leah." Or take it one step further and name as many generations as you can: "I am Shari, daughter of Judy, daughter of Vivian, daughter of Dora, and mother of Alex and Erica. I give my hand to you, my sister (take the hand of the woman next to you)." Surrogate mothers or other important mother figures in one's life can also be honored by being named. This ritual is inspired by my matrilineal Jewish heritage.

Naming is a lovely spiritual twist on introductions; it is also a potent way to remind ourselves of the interconnectedness of all women, from generation to generation, and of the fact that we were all borne by another woman, who was borne by another woman, who was borne by another woman…It seems fitting to start a Blessingway by paying tribute to the women who mothered us, recognizing our place in the line of mothers before us and honoring the timelessness of the work of birth and motherhood.

Appreciation rituals focus on the people who are present at the Blessingway ceremony. The mother-to-be may introduce each friend or relative to the group, describe the person's relationship to her, and express why she holds that person dear. Alternatively, each woman may introduce herself, explain her personal connection to the mother-to-be, and share what she appreciates most about her. Verbalizing what you cherish about each other gives you the opportunity to put into words the love that is already in your hearts.

Appreciations set a positive and deeply personal tone, thereby opening the door to greater intimacy within the group. Appreciations can also be a meaningful way to end a Blessingway ceremony, with the honoree acknowledging and thanking each person for the tangible and intangible gifts she has given on this day and every day.

My Blessingway gave me a lot of food for thought. I had been having a lot of fears about not being able to be the perfect mother of two. I had also been processing the fact that I was not perfect even as the mother of one, and that my mother had not been perfect either…that each of us was just human, with our own struggles and faults. At my Blessingway, I came to the realization that no one person can meet all the needs of any other person, and that that's okay. When we each introduced ourselves by naming our mothers and surrogate mothers, I realized that even though my mother herself hadn't given me everything I needed growing up — like consistent nurturing and protection — that I had had many mothers and really my needs had been met.

— Michelle

Naming really highlights the connection with your past and the concept of lineage, especially if your own mom is there.

— Donna

It's so rare that you're in a situation when 15 people tell you what they appreciate about you, and to hear all that at once is overwhelming. I liked it. And everybody was so genuine. I was surprised by some of the depth of what people expressed.

— Barbara

I had people go around the circle and introduce themselves, describing their connection with Gloria. I asked them: how did you meet Gloria, what drew you to her, and why is she so important to you? I hadn't anticipated that that would be as emotional as it was; people really said some beautiful things about what they loved about her and there were lots of tears. It took a really long time because each person had a lot to say.

— Bobbi

A Blessingway Bracelet

Gathering for a Blessingway sends a strong message of love, support, and togetherness. The Blessingway bracelet adds a concrete visual symbol of our interconnectedness — to each other, to women throughout history, and to Mother Earth.

Begin the Blessingway bracelet with everyone seated in a circle. Pass a ball of yarn or thread from woman to woman, starting and ending with the pregnant mother.

Any color will do, but red is often chosen because of its symbolism, representing love, the feminine spirit, and the mystery of female vitality (we bleed monthly yet we do not die from it). Pearly white or blue also work nicely to evoke images of the umbilical cord.

My circle of friends has settled on cotton macramé thread as the most comfortable and durable choice, but wrap it loosely because it will shrink when it gets wet, as will cotton yarn. My sister prefers silk cord, as it is beautiful, inexpensive, and quite strong. Handspun wool is lovely, but it may irritate people with sensitive skin or allergies. Hemp twine must be washed in soap and water first to avoid causing itchiness; it may also be weak unless several strands are braided together, and it will stretch when it gets wet.

As you pass the ball of yarn or thread around the circle, each woman can use it as a "talking stick" while it is in her hands — a traditional way of giving the speaker permission to speak for as long as she wishes, with the assurance of uninterrupted attention from the entire group. She may demonstrate the completion of her turn by winding the yarn around her wrist two or three times and then handing the ball to the next person in the circle.

Other rituals may also be incorporated. For example, each person could present the mother with beads for a necklace, add a flower to an ivy headwreath, and/or share a special reading before wrapping the yarn around her wrist and passing the ball along to the next person.

Punctuate the transition from one person's turn to the next with a short chant, drumming, or the ringing of a bell or gong. Or, let that time-space be filled with silence.

At the end of the Blessingway ceremony, the yarn can be cut in the gaps between neighbors, with the remnants being tied around each woman's wrist. This service is usually performed for each woman by the woman on her left (the side of receptivity and intuitiveness), who ties the yarn onto her left wrist, ankle, or finger.

Each person may wear her strand like a friendship bracelet until the birth of the baby, when the bracelets may be ceremonially cut (like an umbilical cord). The bracelets will prompt everyone to think of the expectant mother often. For her, the bracelet will be a daily reminder of her Blessingway, of everyone's love and good wishes for her and her baby, and of the strength of her circle of support.

In *A Blessingway*, Cynthia Burke suggests this lovely alternative to the Blessingway bracelet: During a Naming ritual, pass a ball of yarn around so every woman can knot the yarn as she names herself and each of her ancestors. Then tie the ends of the yarn chain together to form a circle symbolic of the circle of life and the interconnectedness of everyone in the group.

This prayer, offered in Moon, Moon *by Anne Kent Rush, is a beautiful introduction to the creation of the Blessingway bracelet.*

<u>As Women Have Always Woven</u>
As women have always woven,
so we weave this yarn into the circle of our lives.
As women have always woven time and the fates,
so let us weave this yarn into the circle of our lives.
As women have always woven the seeds with the earth,
so let us weave this yarn into the circle of our lives.
As women have always woven baskets and tools,
so let us weave this yarn into the circle of our lives.
As women have always woven threads into clothing and shelter,
so let us weave this yarn into the circle of our lives.

As women have always woven words into poetry,
so let us weave this yarn into the circle of our lives.
As women have always woven, so we weave this yarn
with the Goddess who is here with us.
The Goddess is always with us.
As each woman weaves the yarn around the woman next to her,
let her call on the Goddess to be with her in daily life.
Let us all answer, "Goddess be with us."

Note: The word *Goddess* can be replaced with *Great Spirit*, *Mother Earth*, *God Above* or whatever else feels appropriate.

Tying into the circle emphasized the importance of community for me and the baby, and reminded me that the baby would be just fine even if I wasn't perfect — because of that community. That's probably the best gift I could give my kids.   — Ellen

Sometime after my Blessingway, I was in yoga class. I was looking around and I noticed all these purple pieces of yarn around people's wrists and I thought, "Oh, that's for me!" It made me feel so special.   — Ann

Candlelighting

Candles are magical, mystical mood-setters. Since light symbolizes life in so many cultures, they are apropos for an event celebrating birth. Lighting candles creates an atmosphere of reverence, and burns away negativity. Candlelighting can also play an important ceremonial role during a Blessingway.

One ritual option is to light a rainbow of candles as you verbalize the significance of each. In *Celebrating with Ceremony*, Carine Fabius shares the following symbolism for the mother and her baby: "Red is for life, vitality and luck; blue is for health, spiritual development, and protection; green is for fertility, prosperity, and a gain of money; golden yellow is for intellectual development and strength of mind; pink is for love, romance, friendship and happiness; orange is for optimism and success; white is for psychic development, dispelling of negative influences and protection."

Illustration by Marci Tarre

Another option is to invite the pregnant mother to light a double candle. As the wick burns, the joined candles will be separated, just as she and her baby will be separated when their umbilical cord is cut. With this ritual, the mother can symbolically demonstrate her readiness to do the birthwork of transforming mother-with-child into mother and child.

My friend Glenda provided Blessingway participants with a selection of colorful bits of beeswax, asking everyone, as they entered the circle, to select a piece to warm and soften in their hands. Then each person added her bit of color to a large beeswax birth candle during the Appreciations ritual.

Another candlelighting option is to ask each participant to light a small votive candle from the flame of a larger candle, perhaps one that is homemade, has a meaningful scent or color, or has been carved and decorated especially for the occasion. Each person might state a wish for the mother and baby — such as "peace" or "joy" — as she lights a candle.

An attractive pie plate, shallow bowl, or casserole dish filled with sand can hold several candles at once. Adorn this candleholder with flowers, shells, colored sand, or other decorations. Then, consider arranging the candles in a spiral or a circle, as these shapes are especially evocative of female power and positive energy. If your group is small, you could use a candelabra instead to symbolically unite all the candles.

Carving candles with inspirational messages can give the mother encouragement, strength and blessings to carry with her into labor and beyond. Soft beeswax candles are easiest to carve. Carving tools can include such household utensils as shishkabob skewers, Swiss army knives, and corkscrew points. Each person can bring a carved candle from home, or engrave a candle during the Blessingway.

After the Blessingway, the mother can take the candles home to light again when labor begins — as a lovelight, reminiscent of your love and support. The candles will also serve as an automatic reminder to keep the lighting dim in her labor space, which will help labor progress more effectively.

If you all expect to be in close communication with the mother, you may each take one votive candle home to light in support of her when she is in labor. Knowing that all those candles will be burning on her behalf will be a source of strength for her as she labors.

Another candlelighting alternative is a cake-time ritual that gives each person the opportunity to light a candle on the cake. The honoree may wish to say a few words to each person who lights a candle; people may respond either impromptu or by sharing a prepared reading.

Once all the candles are lit, you can sing "Happy Birthday" with the emphasis on the word "birth," or select a ritual song honoring the mother. To emphasize the support of the group, you may all blow the candles out together. Or, to evoke the birthing power within the pregnant woman, she may blow out the candles by herself, with her own life-giving breath.

> Candlelighting raises power and draws the room together. When I had more than 15 candles all going with the same intention — safe journey, successful adoption, healthy baby — I really feel that made a major difference.
> — Barbara

One of the things Carrie felt was wrong with her labor last time was that everybody in the world knew that she was in labor, and she also invited a lot of people to be at her birth. It gave her a sort of paralyzing performance anxiety. So this birth she said, "no one is going to know when I'm in labor, and the only people who are going to be there are my family and my midwife." We decided that for the Blessingway we would all give her candles and we would decorate them and carve our names into them so she would know who they were from. She could burn them when she felt she needed our strength, or to know that we were there in spirit, without having our physical presence or our mental presence of knowing that she was in labor.

— Karen

Readings

Readings give people an opportunity to share wisdom, wit, and insight about pregnancy, birth and parenting. Readings can include poems, prayers, favorite quotes, songs, missives addressed to the mother personally, and even performance art. Some people may prefer to write their own, while others would rather quote from other sources. Encourage people to define "readings" as creatively as they like!

Readings can be shared orally. You may pass around a talking stick, rattle, rainstick, shell, stone, or gourd to pass around; each person can do whatever feels right when she is holding it, whether that means remaining silent, sharing a formal reading, speaking her heart or expressing herself in other ways such as through song. Be sure to give the honoree a chance to speak too, if the spirit moves her.

Sharing readings can take a surprisingly long time, often an hour or more. Many women plan Blessingways with an open-ended finish time to ensure that everyone will feel free to meander through this ritual. Others set specific guidelines limiting each person's speaking time.

One Colorado woman gathered copies of everyone's readings to put into an album for the mother. She also included photos from the Blessingway. If you plan to make a keepsake collection, let people know what the specifications are (e.g. paper size) for any contributions. Alternatively, mail each person one scrapbook page to prepare in advance, then bestow the pages and assemble the scrapbook at the Blessingway ceremony. Women who wish to be present in spirit but are unable to attend in person can also be invited to send album contributions or completed scrapbook pages, which you can present to the mother-to-be on their behalf.

Marcy's mother wasn't able to be there, so she e-mailed me something she wanted read, about the unpredictability and spontaneity of birth and the joy that is possible in that.
— Dana

I lost a baby before I became pregnant with my son. Out of some superstition, I guess, I was just not able to deal with things until I knew that this baby would be here to use them. So I asked people not to bring baby gifts, but to bring pieces of writing to help me in the liminal space between not being a mother and being a mother, and in my journey in labor. I asked them to share something to help usher me into this next phase of life.
— Stefanie

We put the pregnant woman near us or make it feel like she's on our laps and read her stories. People bring storybooks, children's books that they love.
— Nancy

Each woman took a turn to present me with readings or songs or poems with real meaning about motherhood, womanhood, family, and childbearing and those kinds of things. And because it was so open emotionally, everything touched me very deeply and I found deep meaning in each thing people had brought.
— Melisa

They presented me with a book — inside was a letter or note from everyone that was there — that I have to this day. There are times where I've struggled, and I would go back and read these letters that all the women wrote me and it would just give me so much courage and so much strength, and just remind me that all of these other women are supporting me as a woman.
— Karen

Storytelling

For thousands of years, stories have been a powerful way for women to share inspiration and wisdom with each other. However, most of us spend less time than our ancestors sitting together, or working side-by-side, and telling tales. In place of that oral tradition of storytelling, we read books, watch television and movies, or surf the Internet; but those media do not have the intimacy and personalizing touch of family and friends. A Blessingway is a forum in which the old storytelling tradition can be renewed.

Sharing stories is likely to be more fluid and interactive than the presentation of readings described above. An open-ended time can be set aside for telling tales about the surprises, the joys, the courage, or the humor in each person's birth, parenting, or other life experiences. Or, storytelling can be more ritualized, especially if you ask everyone to prepare a story in advance.

Consider passing a talking stick around the circle during storytelling time, or simply place it on the floor in the center of the room so each woman can reach for it whenever she is moved to tell her story.

Because of the potency of the spoken word, I strongly advise you to steer storytelling in a positive direction. Be explicit about the need to ensure an encouraging and affirmative atmosphere throughout the taletelling time. There are many ways to accomplish this: clearly state on the written invitations that it is essential to stay positive; take time pre-ceremony to discuss the importance of protecting the mother from disheartening energy and imagery; choose your words carefully when you initiate the storytelling, perhaps emphasizing that this is a time to share special and positive memories of pregnancy, birth and parenting; or give gentle guidance when people's stories stray into negative territory. Another alternative would be to focus the storytelling specifically on the humorous side of pregnancy, becoming a parent, or mothering. Laughter brings positive energy with it.

Like readings, written versions of everyone's stories can be gathered into a keepsake album for the mother.

We sat around the fire on the beach. We told birth stories and looked at the stars.

— Maura

We talked about what my hopes were, what my fears were. And everyone went around the room and talked about what their hopes were for me, and then it just went into this trading of stories — talking about parenthood, or talking about our own childhood. That was toward the end of my Blessingway, so it naturally segued out of the ritual into a just-sitting-around-talking kind of gathering.

— Melanie

They sang "Happy Birth-Day" and we ate cake. Then we sat around and chatted, and spontaneously in the course of the conversation, each of these experienced mothers gave their own experiences with having babies — things that were hard, things that were most special, things they wish they had thought to ask earlier, like asking for help with breastfeeding or asking people to leave you alone with the baby when you just want some peace and quiet. It was such a gift, to hear their stories. I felt so much better prepared having this advice, this information that I wouldn't have gotten any other way.

— Rachel

Everyone shared a humorous story about her experience of pregnancy, mothering, adoption, becoming a parent. Because Carla had so many difficulties during her pregnancy and still had some unresolved fears, it was especially helpful to be able to find the humor.

— Dana

Beads

Beads are a popular choice as sentimental tokens of affection. One powerful Blessingway ritual is the creation of a personalized necklace for the honoree. Selecting beads for a necklace provides Blessingway participants with the opportunity for creative self-expression, as each bead will impart its own symbolic message. In addition, the necklace you make will serve as a tangible reminder to the mother-to-be that she has a strong circle of support made up of many people who love her and her baby. It is also a reminder that there is beauty in birth and that every birth, like every necklace, is unique.

Usually, everyone is asked to bring one or more special beads to contribute. Put a selection of extra beads up for grabs, to avoid the awkwardness of someone being left out because she forgot to bring any. Or, supply all the beads yourself; fill a beautiful bowl with beads that you know will appeal to the honoree or be meaningful to her, then let each person choose one or more of those beads to add onto the necklace. I encourage you to invite the honoree to bring any beads that she would like to add to her own necklace. If she has been using affirmations to prepare for the birth, she may wish to share them aloud at her Blessingway, adding one bead to her necklace as she verbalizes each affirmation.

The mother-to-be may draw strength from wearing her necklace daily until her baby is born, or she may prefer to hang it on the wall or include it in a birth altar. Hannah said she displayed her necklace on the baby's dresser along with some other special items, then "I put it on on my due date as a sort of welcoming, and I wore it all the way through labor. I even put it on as a sort of protective amulet a few days later when I had to leave her for the first time."

Maria donned the beaded necklace when labor began, as a symbol of her acceptance that it was time to give in and let her body's wisdom take over to birth her baby. Her midwife recounted, "When I walked in, that's what I saw — big naked Maria… wearing her necklace. It was the most incredibly powerful image!"

The Birth Necklace

Illustration by Sandra Greenstone

Practical Hints

⚬ Make a necklace, not a bracelet. Most women find bracelets restrictive and uncomfortable to wear in late pregnancy, especially if they experience a lot of swelling.

⚬ Select a thread that will be sturdy and tangle-free. My local jewelry store recommends several options:

> ⚬ Nylon cord — For small-holed beads, choose one that is stiff enough to use without a needle
> ⚬ Upholstery thread — You may need a needle
> ⚬ Flexible wire — Be careful not to let it get bent before stringing the beads
> ⚬ Hemp thread — But it must be washed first so it does not cause itchy skin
> ⚬ Satin cord — If any trinkets cannot be strung directly onto the cord, securely tie them on with thread. Use a matching color if you do not wish for the thread to show

⚬ Specify large-holed beads on the invitations, and/or taping on a sample of the chosen cord or thread to ensure that everyone will bring usable beads.

⚬ Provide extra-long thread and choose a clasp that is easy to remove and reattach, so the recipient can easily adjust the length or rearrange the order of the beads to make her necklace more comfortable and/or more visually pleasing.

⚬ Use square knots to tie off the necklace or secure the clasps. Clear nail polish or Elmer's glue can be used to strengthen your knots.

⚜ If the expectant father will be included in the ceremony, consider Robin Sale's suggestion in "Creating a Blessing Way Ceremony" to present him with a necklace of colored corn, a common symbol of fertility. It is easy to string corn kernels with needle and thread, once they have soaked in water for 24 hours.

Photo by Cindy Wauer

For my Blessingway, I was asked to bring beads for a necklace, and to bring an affirmation for each of them. What was really neat was that I said the affirmations and then everybody said them back to me, which was also this really powerful re-affirmation. I didn't just put it out there; it was acknowledged and supported and I had to accept it back. I wasn't just affirming myself, but was being affirmed by a community of women.

— Melisa

They brought beads and each woman presented her beads and what they meant to her, what they symbolized, and I strung them. I wore that necklace daily between the Blessingway and when I gave birth, and actually I had it on during labor. It really held a lot of hope in it for me.

— Pam

My friend was in the middle of childbirth with her second or third child and things just weren't coming together. Then she says she went into the bedroom and put on the birth necklace, the necklace she had received at her Blessingway, and the baby was born within twenty minutes! She said she's never had such a powerful birth experience. What I'm talking about is the power of the support. To have some objects or beads at the birth to wear or that are somehow in her visual experience...reminds her of that support, that caring. There's something about being held, even psychically, by a group of women, especially women who have given birth, that sets something in motion for the birth process that may not have been there before.

— Sandra

I've been to a number of births where women have worn that necklace and it's been the only thing on their body when they give birth, and it's very powerful. I know that occasionally they're looking at it or they're touching it or feeling it. But also beyond the physical touchstone reminder, there's this sense that what they're doing is now elevated, that there are all these women out there that know she's approaching this. They're with her in spirit. So I have to say, have I seen a difference? Yes, there's a little bit of calm, a little bit of knowingness.

— Mickey

Gifts from the Heart

Heartfelt gifts from loved ones — from a simple feather found on the front lawn to an elaborate hand-stitched quilt — are great treasures. Their sentimental value is immeasurable, as they carry the givers' affectionate messages within them forever. Ritualizing the presentation of such Gifts from the Heart emphasizes that a Blessingway is focused on the pregnant mother and on meeting her spiritual and emotional needs.

Establish a leisurely pace for the intimate exchange of Gifts from the Heart. Every gift-giver will need ample, unhurried time to speak about her gift and its symbolism. There may be long stretches of thoughtful silence, or there may be tears of happiness as the honoree realizes how much her friends and relatives love her and wish her well. Be sure to give the mother-to-be the opportunity to express herself too; she may use this time to share a reading, vocalize her fears and concerns, reminisce about what the last nine months have meant to her and her family, or give a small token of love and thanks to everyone else.

Most commonly, Gifts from the Heart are arranged into a ceremonial display or Blessingway altar. I will use the word "altar" here to refer to both religious and secular collections of particular objects that have deep personal meaning for the expectant mother, such as a photo of her husband, a pile of seashells, a fertility doll, or a rainbow of candles bestowed upon her in her Blessingway circle.

Visually connecting with these objects can spiritually sustain the mother throughout her pregnancy and labor, and after the birth. Because the altar embodies love and ceremonial significance, the mother draws strength, courage, and inner tranquility from it. Her family may find it to be a source of comfort and encouragement as well.

The mother may initiate her own altar, or you may create an altar on her behalf. Place a few special items on it before the ceremony begins, then during the Blessingway ceremony, ask each participant to add a token that is symbolic of her love and blessings for the mother and child. For the presentation of altar contributions, a rattle can be used as a talking stick; it may be held in the left hand of the speaker and shaken to awaken thoughts from within, suggests Nan Koehler.

Lay the altar out on any flat surface such as a table, a bedroom dresser, a beautiful cloth, or a receiving blanket (new or used by other babies the mother knows and loves). If toddlers will be participating in the ceremony, make sure the altar is either child-friendly or out of reach. You can make a more permanent altar by using grout to spackle talismans to a small table.

Ideally, the Blessingway altar will be readily accessible to the mother at any time, so she can always return to the beneficent energy of the people who cherish her. If the Blessingway is held in the intended birthplace, the altar can remain right where it is created. Otherwise, make it easy for the mother to transport to her home, and then to the hospital or birth center when she is ready to give birth.

Customizing a dreamcatcher, wreath, hanging branch, or mobile is another alternative. Just like altars and necklaces, these are visual reminders of love and strength, made collectively by all the Blessingway participants.

According to Deborah Jackson in *With Child*, in the Zulu tradition, decorations adorn the birthplace so that the baby is sure to see beauty from the moment of birth. Hung in the birthing room and later in the child's room, they can also serve as protective amulets during pregnancy, labor, and birth, and for years after the baby is born. At one Michigan Blessingway, after each person tied a trinket representing her blessing for the baby onto a wreath, the mother-to-be was given instructions to untie them at a certain age and bestow them ceremonially upon the child.

It is unusual these days to forego store-bought gifts when celebrating the coming of a baby; when tokens of sentiment are given at all, it is usually in addition to material purchases. Therefore, if you are planning a Gifts from the Heart ritual, you will probably need to explain your intention clearly in the invitations, using such phrases as:

- ⚜ Please bring gifts that are handmade, handed down, or handpicked for Gina and/or Baby Martinez
- ⚜ Symbolic gifts from nature only
- ⚜ Heartfelt gifts
- ⚜ Please spend your time and love instead of your money on Nancy's gifts

⚜ Something handmade, found, or brought from home that you wish to share with Julianna

⚜ "Talismans...that mean something special..., items that represent strength, good-will and courage." (from *Water Birth*, by Susanna Napierala)

⚜ Something that is meaningful to you in your relationship with Natalie, or something that symbolizes pregnancy or motherhood or your wishes for her during her birth

⚜ Small tokens of sentiment only

Instead of excluding typical shower gifts, some hosts simply facilitate setting aside the more material gifts for the mother to open after the ceremony, either with the group or privately.

Sometimes the pregnant woman will present symbolic items to everyone who attends her Blessingway. For example, Bronwen recounts, "Each woman who came to Kira's Blessingway received a moonstone which she would keep in sacred trust, to hold the energy of the Blessingway and our good wishes for Kira during the birth. And she had one, and she gave one to her husband." Reciprocal gift exchanges, where the mother-to-be both gives and receives gifts in a ceremonial fashion, can underscore the cyclical nature of love.

> We asked them to bring a token of their blessing, from the heart. So right from the beginning, people had the idea that it was going to be a more spiritual experience than just going to Toys-R-Us and buying a plastic toy.
> — Kathi

> Everyone presented me with Gifts from the Heart — special things that they had made or chosen especially for me. They went around the circle, with each person presenting her gift and taking time to explain the meaning behind it. Grandmomma gave me the quilt from her own bed, saying that her mother had made it when she was first pregnant, and all her babies had slept under it with her when they were little, so she wanted to pass that legacy along. Gran had made a tape recording of

herself singing "power" songs, songs honoring women and mothers, lullabies in English and Russian, and psalms. Mom gave me a little statue of a mother and child gazing adoringly into each other's eyes; she wished many such magical moments upon me in my mothering years to come. Jeanine presented me with a sugar-maple leaf and a promise to plant the whole tree in the backyard as a symbol of my womanly strength and the sweetness of motherhood. Siri handpainted flowers and goddess icons onto a hollow gourd, representative of the fertility of my womb. Noreen brought a piece of coral to serve as a protective amulet. Liz passed along a stone with the word "trust" engraved upon it that had made its way around our circle from birthing woman to birthing woman for several years, along with a certificate of provenance (listing the order of past possession). Stacy, my lifelong friend, surprised me with the dollhouse dolls we had played with together as children. Ann presented me laughingly with a welcome mat and a full sugarbowl (as a symbol of sweetness). My other friends brought things I could use to pamper myself, like homemade massage oils and bath salts. — Amanda

Someone made a pouch for everyone to put a good luck charm in. Linda also added some things. Then it was her husband's job when she was in labor to hold the bag!

— Jennifer

We set up an altar and on that altar we represented the four elements. Carrie put things on it that represented power to her, that were important to her. Then I invited all of the guests to bring something of their own power to place on the altar during the ceremony to also give Carrie strength.

— Karen

Setting up the altar brings the abstract concept of the four directions into concrete form. We place flowers in the center.

In the East we place a green or yellow candle and a feather, perhaps some incense or a musical instrument symbolizing the air element. A feather or instrument is also passed around when calling the East. Air represents the sunrise, infancy, dawn, illumination, male energy, the eagle.

In the south, we place a bowl of food. This is passed around clockwise and eaten when the Spirit of the South is invoked. Here we put a yellow or red candle. This color together with the food symbolizes the fire element: midday, hot sun, childhood, youthful sexuality, laughter, innocence, the mouse.

The West brings water, represented by a cup of tea which is passed around at the appropriate time. Here is also placed a black candle and a shell with water in it (water that comes from a powerful source, such as the ocean, if possible) representing the water element: sunset, maturation, the dreamkeeper, emotions, female energy, changes, introspection, our tears, autumn, harvest, the bear.

In the North, we often place a bowl of salt which is passed around and tasted when the North is called. The candle color is white, representing the earth element: old age, crystals, stones, earth, clay, winter, old age, darkness, night, the end of a cycle, wisdom, the horse or buffalo.

Hymea Storm, author of *Seven Arrows*, says we start the circle in the

North seeking wisdom, head for the South, innocence, enter our subconscious dream state, the West, and end up in the East, illuminated!

These are examples of how we *might* represent the four directions. Each group, each woman, each circle is unique.

— Nan Koehler, from "Blessingway (California Style)"

Stephanie had made this wheel out of grapevine and put little different colored pieces of ribbon and yarn on it. She had instructed people to bring a token of their blessing for the baby, to tie onto that "Blessingway Wheel." So then there was this time of going around the circle where each person would offer their blessing and talk about what they brought and tie it onto the wheel.

Somebody had made a little clay figure of a clown and tied that on and said that they hope the baby always has a sense of lightheartedness and laughter in his life. Somebody else had written a little poem about having strength and courage throughout life, and that was in the form of a little scroll that was tied on with a ribbon. Some people brought things from nature — a feather, a seashell, a rock — and talked about a connection with the earth or with the sea and giving that blessing to the baby. One woman brought a string of tiny kites; she said no matter how intense things get, always take time to go fly a kite! Parenting and growing as a child, there are going to be tough times, and there's going to be dissention, and there are going to be arguments, so that was one of my favorites. Now that I have teenagers, I really draw on that.

— Kathi

People brought flowers — whether dried, or fresh that would dry — to put onto a "Blessingway Wheel" to give the blessing of beauty throughout the baby's life. The mother hung it where she could see it during her labor and draw on those blessings and the strength of that circle, and now it belongs to the baby.

— Joanna

Wishes for Baby

Although the central focus of a Blessingway is generally on the spiritual journey of the expectant mother, it can be meaningful to include a baby-centered ritual too.

One such ritual is the collection of wish cards from everyone, including perhaps the mother herself. Ask "What do you wish for this baby?" Each woman can write her thoughts on a an attractive notecard, sign her name, and place the card in a designated vessel. Share the wishes aloud first, or simply collect the cards for the mother to read privately at a later time.

Be creative in your choice of paper and writing utensils. I like silky handmade paper or colorful cardstock and a selection of markers and calligraphy pens. Acid-free paper and pens will make the cards longer-lasting, as you will avoid the yellowing and crumbling that typically happens when paper ages. Provide plenty of extra cards and/or scrap paper so people can write a couple of drafts before finalizing their cards.

Any wide-mouthed basket, jar, or can will work as a card-collecting vessel. Add ribbons or other decorations to transform a simple container into a beautiful keepsake, suitable for display. Alternatively, gather the wishes into a scrapbook (see Readings, page 86), set out a journal for each person to write in, or tie prayer ties onto a medicine wheel or wreath.

Whether the mother displays it or not, this collection of wishes is sure to have a special place in her heart. She will enjoy rereading everyone's messages both before and after the birth, and then someday she will be able to pass those wishes on to the baby to read and treasure himself.

Wishes can also be represented by symbolic objects and/or spoken words. For example, each person can place a seed into a pouch, then verbally share a wish for the growth of the honoree's family.

"Ken and Marilynn," recounts Jill Hopkins in *Welcoming the Soul of a Child*, "passed around two nylon climbing ropes with different colors. As the ropes came around the circle, each person said a prayer (silently or out loud) and tied a knot into each rope. Ken and Marilynn purposefully guided the ropes behind each person (after the prayer knots were tied) symbolizing how the entire community was included in the birthing of this child. One prayer rope was to be left in their baby's room; the other rope was cut apart at the close of the ceremony. Everyone was then invited to take a knot (containing one of the prayers offered in the ceremony) home with them. Ken and Marilynn's idea was that each person would then become a 'Keeper of the Prayer' — safely keeping and holding close the prayers and blessings offered to their unborn child. The knots also symbolically expressed how 'tied' together they all were as a family and a community."

Nancy Wainer, a Massachusetts midwife, prefers to share spoken wishes only. She explains: "We choose one quality that we own, that we are willing to share with the baby. So one woman would say, 'I have a fabulous sense of humor and I'm going to share that by putting that in the basket for the baby.' And somebody else would say, 'I have amazing courage. I've had adversity in my life and while I don't wish adversity on this baby, I wish this baby the courage to meet it if it comes. I have been able to meet some very intense challenges in my life with clarity and wisdom...so I am going to share that piece of me and put courage into the basket.'" Thus, the basket Nancy gives each pregnant woman is full of loving wishes but not objects.

In *The Circle of Life*, Carol Leonard describes another oral tradition in which "each woman in turn [speaks] three blessings: one for the mother, one for the baby, and one for the global community of women."

However you go about it, the chance to express and receive good wishes will be appreciated by everyone involved; it is a rare and welcome opportunity for most of us.

> Underneath the candle, we had an ultrasound picture of the baby, so the group passed that around the circle as each person gave a wish for Gloria and the baby.
> — Bobbi

> What appealed to me was doing something that was ceremonial and a real sharing of wishes for the mother and the baby. I thought that was so much more meaningful, and probably something people really wanted to be able to do. There aren't a lot of venues for people to express those kinds of wishes.
> — Lisa

If you're making prayer ties, say your prayer to her, out loud, looking her in the face. Put your hand on her belly, put your hand on her face, be as loving as humanly possible, and speak your prayer from the heart.

— Gae

I felt very carried on the well wishes of so many people, and I think that made such a major difference.

— Suzanna

Corner Stones

The Corner Stones ritual give a woman courage by symbolically representing the solidity of the community that surrounds and protects her family and her home. Since the Judeo-Christian bible refers to the tradition of marking important events with piles of stones, Corner Stones may also be a religiously or culturally meaningful choice for some women.

To perform a Corner Stones ritual, ask everyone to bring at least one stone to the Blessingway, or provide an ample supply to share. Gather at an outside corner of the honoree's home. With stones in hand, say a blessing, a prayer, or a wish for the pregnant woman, her baby, and her family; this can be done either as a group or individually. Next, place one stone apiece on the ground near the cornerstone of her house. Repeat this ritual at each of the four corners of her home. Or, perform the verbal part of the ritual just one time, then divide the stones into fourths and deposit one pile at each of the four corners.

The stones become a tangible reminder of the strong foundation of love and blessings that will always be there to support her and her family.

Birthing Power Shirts

What a woman wears during her pregnancy can influence and reflect her own pregnant self-image. By giving her a shirt that expresses *power, joy, womanly strength, feminine beauty*, or *encirclement with love*, you can make a positive, confidence-boosting addition to her maternity wardrobe.

Give a special shirt to the mother-to-be ahead of time, to wear on the day of her Blessingway and throughout the rest of her pregnancy. Or, present the shirt ceremonially as part of her Blessingway, and ask her or help her to don it for the rest of the day if she wishes.

Before the Blessingway, a designated person can decorate a roomy, comfortable maternity shirt or an extra-large T-shirt. For a more collaborative approach, you can all create a shirt together as part of the Blessingway ceremony. Let your imagination guide you as you use paints, tie-dye, embroidery, beads, ribbons, indelible fabric markers, or sequins.

Instead of decorating a shirt, just choose one that is made of extra-special fabric such as crushed velvet, or consider purchasing a T-shirt with Harriette Hartigan's lovely pregnancy/birth/baby photography silkscreened onto it. (To order, visit her website at www.harriettehartigan.com)

Alternatively, bestow a favorite maternity shirt of your own upon the expectant mother. Hand-me-downs are a great way to remind a pregnant woman of her connection to and support by other women.

I hope you will encourage the mother to share whatever shirt you give her, passing it along from pregnant woman to pregnant woman as a symbol of love, friendship, support, feminine power and the interconnectedness of mothers everywhere.

> It was really special to have been given this beautiful thing, not to keep, but to borrow for a little while — this heavy velvet patchwork shirt that had been going through our community of women for years, that had been worn by other women who had given birth and faced their fears and joys and motherhood and everything else. — Dana

Crazy Ribbon Hats can be a lighthearted alternative or addition to a Birthing Power shirt. If traditional gifts are being opened, simply attach all the ribbons from the wrappings to an upside down paper plate with pre-attached chin-ties (such as stapled-on yarn or ribbon) and voilá — she has a silly, happy hat to wear for the rest of the Blessingway. If there will be no gifts to unwrap, ask everyone to bring a favorite ribbon from home, or just provide a grab-bag of ribbons and invite each person to choose one to add to the honoree's hat.

Releasing Fears

Pregnancy is a particularly vulnerable time, rife with deep-seated fears. It takes great courage to overcome those fears, let loose, and birth a baby. To help build that courage, you can give the pregnant woman the opportunity to acknowledge, confront, and maybe even embrace her worst fears within the loving circle of the Blessingway.

Once the Blessingway's opening rituals have established an atmosphere of love and unconditional acceptance, and the mother-to-be feels safe and relaxed, you can invite her to verbalize her apprehensions and ambivalences about the birth of her baby. Perhaps other mothers can also share what their own qualms were before birthing their babies.

After the mother has put her fears into words, there are many different ways to help her symbolically release them. In the *Blessing the Way* video guidebook, Laura Scheerer Whitney suggests:

- A healing song or chant or a symbolic "letting go"
- Burning the fears with fire
- Letting the fears drift away in the smoke of a sage stick [or blown-out candle]
- Washing the fears away with a water blessing

   ⚬ Turning the fears into imaginary bees and making a great buzzing noise together as they fly away!

By addressing her innermost fears, the mother is sure to gain confidence in her ability to meet the challenges of pregnancy, birth and parenting. She will also have clarified for herself and for the rest of you what her biggest needs are for emotional support. And, once she has let go of her inhibitions enough to openly express her fears, she will feel more free to accept support whenever she needs it.

> I've done a couple of informal little Blessingways where we've just kind of all gathered around and washed the woman's feet and listened to her talk about her fears. That's a really powerful thing — to just <u>listen</u>.
> — Sandra

> In that safe and loving atmosphere, I finally felt free to express my deepest fear about having this baby. It was such a relief to go into labor without carrying the weight of that heavy secret upon me anymore.
> — Michelle

Belly Masks

Belly mask-making is a sensual art form that honors the creation of life and the bond between mother and child. Three-dimensional belly masks are durable and long-lasting, and provide a stunning way to preserve memories of the pregnancy.

There are many options for incorporating belly masks into Blessingways. You may help the mother to cast one as part of the Blessingway ceremony. Or, if you and the mother cast the mask several days beforehand, everyone at the Blessingway may help decorate it with paints or ornaments such as sequins and feathers.

The belly mask is lightweight enough to hang on the wall as a decoration. Or, it could serve as a vessel to hold the pregnant woman's talismans. My friend Diana saved hers until her son's first birthday, then filled and decorated it with special mementos from his first year. In *Birthing From Within*, Pam England and Rob Horowitz recount how one couple even used their belly mask, padded with a soft sheepskin, as a cradle for their newborn!

However it is used, the belly mask is sure to be an inspiration and a conversation piece for years to come.

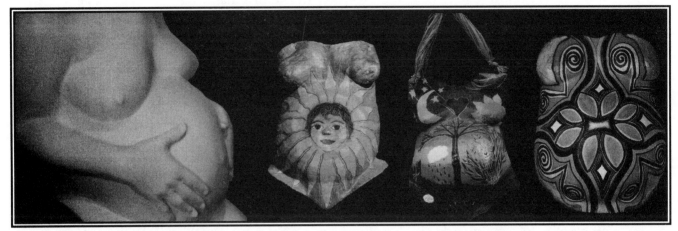

Belly masks and photos by Francine Krause

Preserving Your Shape Shift: Making a Belly Cast
Reprinted with permission from *Birthing From Within*,
by Pam England and Rob Horowitz.

What you will need:
 ⚘ Oil, water-soluble jelly and/or a thin layer of cotton quilt batting or cotton pre-casting padding (used to wrap a fractured extremity before casting; can be bought at a medical supply store).

 ⚘ Fast-drying (5 - 8 minutes) plaster bandages (used to make casts for broken bones, they're inexpensive and can be bought at medical supply stores). Get eight (2 or 3 inch) rolls to cast just breast and belly, or 12 rolls if you include shoulders, upper arms, and upper 1/3 of thighs. If you buy 4 or 6 inch rolls, use less.

⚴ Plastic tablecloth, old shower curtain or a drop cloth to protect the floor.

⚴ A cake pan of hot water — to dip strips of plaster bandages in.

⚴ Art supplies to decorate the belly cast:

⚴ Plaster of Paris: if you want to smooth the original rough gauze surface; and to enhance features such as nipples or belly button, as well as strengthen the cast.

⚴ Wire mesh "sandpaper" to get a really smooth plaster surface.

⚴ Gesso, paint, colored tissue paper, feathers, beads, pictures or photos to collage, and so on.

⚴ Shellac to seal and preserve your creation.

Mother: Choose Your Pose

Standing, or sitting on the edge of a seat, will result in a round, more full-bodied sculpture. Experiment with various poses: lean forward, to one side or back, or against the wall — find the shape/pose you want to preserve. Assume a position in which you can remain fairly still for about twenty minutes. DON'T LIE DOWN *(this position produces a flattened breast-belly sculpture)*.

What to Do: Getting Ready

Sculptor:

1. Put on old clothes or an apron and roll up your sleeves. You might want to take off jewelry.

2. Cover the floor with a drop cloth. Make sure room is warm but well-ventilated.

3. Cut the plaster bandages into strips approximately 6, 10, and 14 inches long.

4. Generously apply lubricant to the mother's breast, belly (neck/arms/thighs), *going no more than halfway* around her sides and just above the pubic hair. If necessary, use cotton padding to cover armpit, belly, or pubic hair. (If you don't use enough lubrication or padding, remind the mother to use one of her pain techniques as her hair is being pulled out when the cast comes off!)

Making the Cast

1. Fill the pan with warm water.
2. Glide *one plaster strip at a time* through the water for a few seconds. Never let go of the strip, keeping it taut, open and flat. (DON'T LET IT FOLD OR TWIST ON ITSELF.)
3. With the short (6 inch) strips you can gently squeeze out excess water by running your index and middle fingers down the strip.
4. Apply the strip to the mother's body. Smoothing and overlapping the strips in various directions strengthens the body cast.
5. WORK QUICKLY because the plaster begins to set (dry), and the cast begins to separate from her body about 10 - 15 minutes after you begin.
6. The cast will be ready to remove about five minutes after you are finished casting. Have the mother help loosen it further by doing a little "belly dance" to help loosen the cast as you ease it off at the edges.

Finishing Touches

The body cast will need 48 hours to dry completely before you begin decorating it. (If it's not thoroughly dry before you seal the outside with gesso, paint or shellac, the inner layers may begin to mold.)

Before painting or decorating, smooth the surface of the cast by dry-walling it with a pasty mixture of plaster of Paris or paint it with gesso. (Gesso is a white, durable paint-like mixture of plaster used to prepare and smooth the surface of a sculpture before painting.)

There's no end to the decorating possibilities: paint, collage with your baby's photos or magazine cut-outs, tissue paper designs, dried flowers, beads, feathers, or written messages.

After your baby is born, you can add footprints (right where he/she used to kick you under the ribs) on the sculpture with ink or paint,...or make an impression of the footprint in wet plaster on the cast.

When you are finished, you can seal the colors and artwork with shellac.

The website at *www.bellymask.com* (707-824-8357) offers a complete, user-friendly kit with quality materials such as unpetroleum jelly and special body soap. The website also has an online exhibit featuring photos of beautifully painted belly masks created by artist Francine Krause, the originator of the pregnancy belly mask concept.

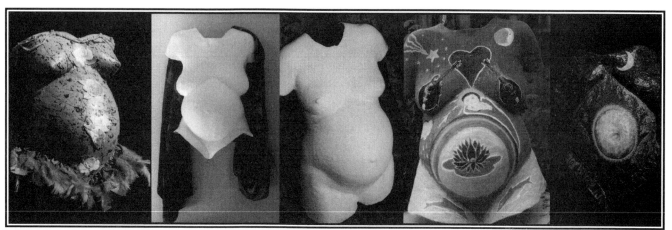

Belly masks and photos by Francine Krause

Quilts

In *Birthing From Within*, Pam England shares the story of a pioneer woman who drew strength, joy, and courage from a handmade baby quilt. What a priceless gift it would be for any mother today to receive a quilt sewn especially for her baby by all the women who love her.

There are many options for quiltmaking. For example, you can prepare a quilt entirely ahead of time, individually or as a group, and present it to her at the Blessingway. If you each make a square, one person can piece all the squares together and bring the quilt to the Blessingway for everyone to help with the final stitching in a quilting bee. Or, you could each create personalized squares right there at the Blessingway using appliqué, fabric paints, or fabric markers; then send all the squares home with one person (possibly the mother herself) to assemble. Each contributor may use indelible ink to sign her name on the square she made. People who are unable to attend the Blessingway ceremony can still share in this gift of love by mailing a quilt square.

If the mother-to-be is already making or planning to make her own quilt, she might like a quilting bee to help assemble her own squares. Or, if she is making a newborn-sized quilt, maybe she would appreciate receiving a toddler-sized quilt and/or a larger one for the baby to grow into someday.

An afghan can take the place of a quilt, with each person knitting or crocheting a square of a predetermined size. Or, consider other forms of collaborative artwork instead, such as creating a collage; building a sculpture; painting a mural on paper, cloth, or a wall; or decorating a cradle or changing table.

Embroidered Diapers and Painted T-Shirts

For a woman who is committed to using cloth diapers for her baby, Courtney Cooke, author of *The Best Baby Shower Book*, suggests taking a few minutes during your gathering for each person to handstitch a simple design onto a cloth diaper or diaper cover. Provide a variety of diaper sizes, thread colors, and embroidery needles. You might offer some basic templates (such as hearts or crescent moons) for the less adventurous sewers in the group, along with fabric pencils for tracing them.

Like a quilting bee, this diaper-embroidering activity engenders the camaraderie that comes from working together. The resulting collection of personalized diapers will be a practical and fun gift.

Mickey and her circle of friends included a similar ritual in their "alternative baby showers" many years ago. They collected babies' T-shirts of all different sizes, then painted them during the festivities. In addition to the fun of sharing such a creative process, they were able to present the expectant mother with a complete layette of individually decorated T-shirts.

Making these special gifts for the baby can add another rich dimension to a ceremony in honor of the mother.

Planting a Tree

Long ago, trees represented children growing between Mother Earth and Father Sky, so tree-planting has ancient symbolic roots.

Ceremonially planting a tree in honor of a new baby can be deeply satisfying for the parents. In addition, children take great pride and pleasure in watching "their" tree grow, helping to tend it, and eventually harvesting its fruit. It gives them a feeling of earthiness, a sense of belonging to nature and its cyclical seasons, and a wondrous understanding and appreciation of the miracles of life.

Planting can be accompanied by a brief statement of thanksgiving, or by a more extensive ceremony. Singing, dancing, prayers, readings, silent meditation, expressing wishes for the baby and libations can all be incorporated as you circle around the tree. Perhaps each person can participate in the planting process in a designated way, such as taking turns with the shovel or helping to place the tree in the ground, pat the earth back down, and water the roots. You may also incorporate the biblical tradition of using stones to memorialize important events by asking each person to contribute a stone to the creation of a rock garden, sculpture, or border around the tree. Returning to the tree for another small ceremony every year on the child's birthday can become a cherished family ritual too.

In some cultures, the placenta is fed to the new mother, to return some of its goodness to her and sustain her after the birth of her baby. The circle of life and regeneration can also be continued by planting the placenta underneath the baby's tree, to nourish it.

Placentas can be frozen until the day of the tree-planting ceremony. Many factors may influence the timing of this ceremony; for example, you might wait until the ground thaws enough for digging, until grandparents or other loved ones are able to be there, or until the baby's first birthday. Women who live in a temporary location, such as a rental apartment, may wait until they establish a more permanent home.

In *With Child*, Deborah Jackson describes a Nigerian tradition of creating a village playground by planting a special grove with one tree for each newborn child; suburban and urban moms might set out to do something similar in a neighborhood park.

Illustration by Amanda Smith

Or, a life-affirming commitment to the future can be signified by planting bulbs or perennial flowers. When the parents are transient, or planting a tree is space-prohibitive for any reason, another option is to plant a large houseplant into a special pot.

If the baby does not live, a tree can be ceremonially planted in eternal loving memory, perhaps with the placenta or the baby's ashes buried under it.

Tree Symbolism

In *With Child*, Deborah Jackson suggests the following tree symbolism:

- Fruit or nut tree — the fruit of the womb

- Ash tree — long life

- Fig tree — wisdom

- Olive tree — peace

- Maple — sweetness and good luck

Or look to your own cultural or religious heritage for guidance. For example, in the Jewish tradition of my family, we would plant a pine tree for a daughter and a cedar tree for a son.

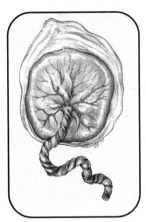

Illustration by Amanda Smith

[The placenta] deserves an honorable burial. Our placenta served Elijah and me beautifully, working hard, willing to die when its work was completed. Holding my placenta, touching it, I am moved to tears by my love and appreciation of it...The two sides of the placenta look quite different. The side that faced the wall of my uterus looks meaty...; the side that faced the baby is smooth, except for an embossed image made by veins: the exact image of a tree. The Tree of Life.

— Maren Tonder Hansen, from *Mother-Mysteries*

We knew families who planted a tree for every child that was born. So we thought planting a tree would also be a fitting memorial for Lucy. We just chose a beautiful tree because she will always be beautiful to us, and we gathered around, with my sister and Grandma and Grampa and the kids, and we said a few prayers as we planted it. It was hard, everyone cried a lot, but it definitely felt good and right to be doing it.

— Alicia

Prayer Showers

The Christian prayer shower concept can be used by members of all faiths to bring a more religious focus to the sharing of inspirational words, wisdom and love.

A religious woman's circle of friends and family may gather together specifically to pray for her and her baby. The emphasis at a Prayer Shower is on helping the expectant or new mother reaffirm her faith in her God at this major crossroads in her life; any gifts are peripheral to the more spiritual nature of the gathering.

A prayer shower can include devotionals, or short talks, about pregnancy, birth, motherhood or children. The hosts usually ask one or two participants to prepare a devotional that addresses the particular spiritual needs of the mother-to-be or new mother.

Elizabeth always asks each woman to share a prayer, religious verse, or song from which she has drawn strength herself. Afterward, she collects printed copies into a keepsake album.

Alternatively, Connie Banack, in "Blessing Way Ceremonies: A Celebration," suggests that each woman can select a slip of paper from a basket, read aloud the hope or trait named thereupon, then pray for it on behalf of the mother and/or her baby. The prayers can continue at home as well; participants can each bring their own note home to place in a visible location as a reminder.

Sometimes a representative group from the prayer shower joins the laboring mother at her home, birth center or hospital to pray in close proximity to her. Awareness of the solidarity and beneficent energy of such a prayer vigil can give the mother courage and confidence during her labor. This prayer group also becomes a ready source of celebrants and helpers that can mobilize right after the baby is born.

> It's so important for mothers giving birth to subsequent babies to have a way for the birth of each baby to be welcomed and celebrated. In our culture, we celebrate the firstborn with a baby shower, but we often are less than supportive of the later children — especially for women having a third or fourth or sixth child. A prayer shower can counteract some of the negative vibes and comments moms like me get from society, and give the mother the encouragement she needs.
> — Tina

Physical Touch and Movement

Arches

An arch is reminiscent of a birth canal or a portal into a new world. This is powerfully perfect symbolism for a woman about to give birth or adopt a baby.

In *Moon, Moon*, Anne Kent Rush describes a human archway "conceived from childhood games like London Bridges." At my own Blessingway, Eleanor began by passing through the arch with burning incense. Then, I slowly made my way through the tunnel as they sang to me. As I passed under each pair of arms, those women let go and circled around the outside of the archway to join it again at the far end. It became one continuous tunnel, all the way from the entrance hall to the seat of honor. I felt like I was carried in on a wave of love and friendship. The two lines then flowed apart to form the Blessingway circle.

In *Artemis Speaks*, a midwife adds insight into the meaning behind this kind of passing through the gates. She says, "In many cultures rites of passage contain 3 stages: Initiation (labor — surrender); Transformation (the moment of birth); Rebirth (into an altered existence — mother and child separate). Two women form an arch. The next woman ducks backward into their arch and their arms are brought down around her (this signifies initiation). She is hugged and kissed by both women forming the arch. They turn her around to face forward. Both of them whisper in one of her ears, 'through a woman you were born into this world (transformation), through a woman you are born into this circle.' Then they raise their arms to form the side of the arch she is facing and push her out through it with the other two arms (rebirth). The next woman in line goes through this process and then these two women who have gone through the arch form a second arch next to the first two women and so on until the 'initiation' arch is a long one to duck backward through...When everyone but the pregnant woman...has gone through the two women forming the first arch both go through and then the pregnant woman goes through. This signifies her bond with the chain of ancestral women that she follows through the birth process."

Archways need not always occur at the beginning of a Blessingway ceremony. A closing birth arch can be a transformational way to return the honoree, and everyone else, to the everyday world.

Deborah Goldman combined the arch with additional elements to create a potent culminating ritual for her friend Stefanie's Blessingway. Stefanie recounts: "She began the Blessingway by passing out brightly colored pens and small pieces of paper, then she asked everybody to look at me in silence for a moment or two. So there I was, just sitting there in all my pregnant glory, all eyes upon me. Next she asked them to write something about me, specifically beginning with the phrase: 'I am the one who...' and I was also asked to do that myself. Then she lined everyone up; she was very meticulous about who she put where in the two lines facing one another. She put my mother and grandmother at the head of the line. She asked them to stand quite close together, and I was instructed to walk through the tunnel that they created, very, very slowly. As I passed each one of them they had to lean in and whisper, to say very softly what their phrase had been. Mostly they started with 'I am the one who sees you as...' or 'I am the one who remembers...' As I walked through this quite narrow passage with the breath and the scents of the women around me, and their words, I was a puddle of tears. At the very end, I was asked to say the phrase I had written: 'I am the one who is two.' So in a sense, I had passed through the birth canal. I was so moved and empowered by that experience, just to have received everybody's words. I think I even said at the end, 'Wow, that's not hard, I can do that.' Actually this was new for me because I didn't pass through my mother's birth canal — I was delivered by Cesarean. So it was a very powerful experience."

A trust walk is another time-honored archway ritual in which the pregnant woman is caressed and massaged in a display of maternal affection from the community of women who will support her during this transitional time in her life. It is described by *Pocket Books News* as "a traditional African ritual that symbolizes the support of all the women present for the new mother. To recreate this tradition, the mother-to-be is blindfolded and led between two lines formed by the [other women]. As the mother walks by, [they] gently touch the woman's shoulders and forehead and take turns hugging her and rubbing her back. This gesture symbolizes the idea that even though a new mother may not know where she is going, she will come to realize that she will be supported and cared for by those around her." The combination of the ritual arch and the blindfold puts a powerful emphasis on physical touch as a means of expressing love.

An ambient arch can serve some of the same purposes as an archway ritual. For example, decorate door moldings or a garden trellis to create a floral archway that the mother-to-be must walk through to enter the Blessingway space. Or, hang a bead curtain in the doorway to symbolize a passageway through the gates of change.

Photo by Therese Langan

I walked through the arch of friendship first and that was really neat because I was able to pass through everyone and connect with each person's face instead of just walking into the room. So that was a really meaningful way to greet and be greeted by everyone there.   — Lynne

I asked everyone to tell Carrie how they see her by finishing the statement: "I am the one who sees you as..." Carrie had no idea that people see her a certain way. It really helped for people to tell her how they saw her. And each time we would tell her we handed her a bead that we had picked out for her and she had it to put on a necklace, so she had all of that energy and all those words with her at her labor. Then at the end, we made a tunnel and had Carrie walk through it, and we whispered all the words that we saw her as, like it was her rite of passage through the "birth canal" into motherhood.   — Karen

 I suppose it could symbolize a baby coming through the birth canal, but it also symbolizes for adoption a real sending out — "okay, go out and get this baby!" — as you travel forth. A sendoff.   — Barbara

Cradling

Cradling uses group touch to send a message of love and support. It requires the full trust of the honoree, as she must let herself be physically lifted, held, and rocked in the arms of loved ones. This is good practice for the challenge of accepting the intimate attentions that will help her get through her labor.

To cradle a woman, you need a minimum of eight people. Six people stand in two rows, with each person grasping the wrists of the person opposite. The honoree is then invited to lie down on top of that strong cradling bed of arms. Finally, someone supports her head and someone else her feet; perhaps her mother or her midwife could play these special roles. Once she is cradled, she is rocked gently side to side. Sing, chant, or play soft music in the background, or rock her in silence. Give her plenty of unhurried time and space to sink into the warmth and comfort of your arms, become physically and symbolically weightless, connect with this sensation that is reminiscent of being cradled in her mother's womb and arms, and feel the absolute security of motherlove.

If Cradling is the closing ritual, consider carrying the mother out as you leave the Blessingway space to symbolize how your love and support will carry her along on her journey through labor and into motherhood.

I was worried about whether she would be comfortable doing the cradling but she really loved it. Usually when people do it they just close their eyes and experience it, but she was more interactive, I think probably because she was a little unsure. But she liked it; she said she couldn't imagine a nicer way to connect with people.   — Bobbi

Most people haven't been lifted up since they were a child. The feeling of being lifted and then cradled and rocked to soft music is a wonderful meditative feeling. Keisha said, "When you're in the delivery room, remember the feeling of all your friends being around you here and lifting you up, supporting you..." It's about trusting, letting other people support you and be there for you.   — Dee

Circle of Love

The Circle of Love combines singing, dancing, and touching into a ritual that infuses and surrounds the pregnant mother with love, protection, and other blessings.
As this ritual is described in *Artemis Speaks*, everyone joins hands, circles around the honoree and chants the following song, adapted from a Sufi one: "May the blessings of her love rest upon you." (*Her love* refers to the Goddess; *God's love* was the original wording. See **Chants, Songs, and Suggested Sources of Music** for the melody.)

With each verse of this chant, or another simple chant of your choosing, one person enters the circle. She places her hands on the pregnant woman, wherever she would like to imbue strength and/or share a quality she feels is strong in herself. This can be a non-verbal channeling of energy, or a naming aloud of the quality you are symbolically giving to the mother.

As one anonymous midwife wrote, "there is a tendency to want to be original ('the person before me put her hands on her heart, I'd better do something else') but give her what you are strong in. Feel your strength flow into her through your hands." You might consider some of the body symbolism she suggests below.

Body Symbolism

Feet — taking her own stance
Thighs — softening and opening
Belly — allowing the transformation
Breasts — being able to nourish
Heart — maintaining her peace
Arms — being able to hold herself together
Hands — grasping her truth
Shoulders — strength to carry the load
Back — not being afraid to see the other side
Head — clarity

A potent way to close the Circle of Love, inspired once again by Sufi tradition, is described by the same midwife: "After everyone has touched the pregnant woman and has returned to the circle, we start moving around as a circle. First as the Full Moon — complete, shining forth, arms in a circle above the head, eyes shining outward, large steps. Then Crescent Moon — left arm arched up, right arm arched down, eyes downcast and hidden, potentiality, enclosed within, small, light, graceful steps. Lastly as Sun — arms straight out to the side, palms outward, eyes straight ahead, firm, strong steps, moving for nothing, adapting to nothing. Shining outward."

The Circle of Love can be finished with a circle dance like this one, a group hug, or the ringing of a bell or gong.

Laying on of Hands

Laying on of Hands is a focused group massage. This ritual of loving touch can bring comfort, strength, and even healing to the mother-to-be. However, Laying on of Hands should not be entered into lightly, as it will concentrate an unimaginable intensity of emotional energy around and within her. (Sort of like labor!) In some cases, this can be an incredibly positive, affirming experience, but in other cases it can be difficult, putting the woman in an uncomfortable or vulnerable position. For this reason, I encourage you to verify that the honoree is receptive before trying Laying on of Hands.

Anyone who has experienced massage knows that there is great energy and power in human touch. When a woman is touched by multiple hands at once, she will feel a surge of energy so strong that it may bring out deep-seated emotions which need to be processed immediately. Thus, before Laying on of Hands is undertaken, the entire circle of women needs to express a willingness to give whatever time and love it will take to support her through her response to the group touch experience.

To do a Laying on of Hands, first designate a chief pair of hands. The chief should be the one whose lead everyone else will follow. She can first ask the mother to lay down in the center of the circle and relax. Or, sit the mother in a comfortable chair where everyone can easily reach to touch her.

Then, before any physical contact is made, the chief should verbalize exactly what you are planning to do and why. She should also lead the group in making an explicit statement of intent, either individually or in unison. For example, each person in turn may repeat, "I will send my love to you and your baby through my touch" or "I am touching you in order to share my woman-power as you prepare to birth your first child."

Once all members of the group have announced their intent, the chief can lay one hand on the mother's body, followed by everyone else simultaneously laying one hand on her, with the other hand resting just off to the side. Guided visualization may be helpful at this point; for example, you can all imagine that you are electrical cords, conducting positive and supportive energy into her body. Everyone's hands will stay gently on the mother's body until the chief removes hers, thereby giving the cue to finish.

Maintain a respectful silence during and after this ritual, giving the mother time to experience your touch and then reengage verbally with the group at her own speed. Alternatively, sing a repetitive song or chant continuously from the time the statements of intent are completed until the time when the mother signals a readiness to move on.

Laying on of Hands can include fathers as well as mothers. Midwife Nan Koehler asks couples to "lay together, spooning, touching as close as possible, making one unit. It's nice if we can do it in their bedroom, on their bed." This electrifying ritual, when done for both partners together, honors the mother, the father, and their union.

If you wish to share the loving touch of the group without the intensity of the Laying on of Hands, Cradling, or Circle of Love rituals, consider ending the Blessingway with a group hug instead. Or, put all your hands on and around the pregnant belly and caress it to convey your blessings and love to the mother and her baby; at the same time, you might sing songs about surrender or opening, or invite the mom to express her thoughts about her readiness for the labor, the birth, and the baby. Another hands-on alternative would be to massage her during the Hairbrushing or Footwashing rituals. Either the person brushing her hair or washing her feet can give her a little massage too, or additional people can be designated to massage particular body parts; meanwhile, the rest of the group can sing, chant, or drum.

Moon Salutations

The moon has long belonged to the female mystical domain. Many traditions honor the moon as a goddess.

Lunar cycles and the concurrent menstrual cycles of women were historically the first reliable markers of the passage of time. Laura Cornell, author of *The Moon Salutation*, noted that romantic pictures throughout history predictably have a full moon in the background, which makes sense because women's ovulation most naturally occurs at the full moon. Under a full moon is when women tend to be at their most open, both sexually and in terms of receptivity to other people and ideas. Women are similarly emotionally and spiritually open during pregnancy, when their bellies grow in roundness like the moon and their skin may shine with a glow that resembles moonlight.

The moon goes through cyclical phases, from fullness to invisibility to fullness again and again, with each phase carrying its own inherent beauty and power. "The moon is ever-changing, yet always whole — like a woman," observed Cornell.

Cornell describes the Moon Salutation as a flowing series of yoga postures that honors femininity by paying tribute to the moon as a female spiritual icon. According to Cornell, the Moon Salutation was first created in 1989 by a group of Kripalu women as a way for all women — including those who are pregnant, menstruating, and menopausal — to honor their female power points.

Many women find that multiple slow-paced repetitions of the Moon Salutation center the body, quiet the mind, and infuse the spirit with a sense of inner strength and woman-power. Some of the postures are cooling, while others are expansive, opening the hips and the chest. The Goddess Pose is aptly reminiscent of birthing postures. You will probably all find the slow, deep breathing that accompanies the movement in this yoga series to be relaxing and refreshing, and the pregnant mother may also find that it replenishes her energy, just as deeper breathing will do when she is in labor.

Like dancing or praying together, repeating the Moon Salutation together is sure to foster a sense of community within your group and strengthen the bond of shared experience. Moon Salutations can be particularly evocative when done in a circle.

There is immense visual impact in such synchronicity of movement, especially with the added continuity that a circle creates. If space doesn't permit a circular formation, consider facing each other in rows in order to maintain a visual connection for everyone.

The following variation of the Moon Salutation series requires no yoga experience whatsoever. With a little practice, you will easily gain enough comfort to be able to guide everyone through it at the Blessingway. Experiment with your own adaptations and/or add music. Consider including selections which the mother has expressed a desire to listen to during labor.

Moon Salutation (Variation)

- ◉ Start with Mountain pose, standing straight and tall and loose, with shoulders back and down, so you feel simultaneously strong and comfortable. Hold this position for several breaths, until the music moves you.
- ◉ Trace the full moon up to Temple position as you inhale.
- ◉ Become the crescent moon as you exhale to the left.

- Inhale back up through the center (Temple), and then exhale to the right.
- Return to Temple with the next inhalation.
- Spread wide to become the Goddess as you exhale. Place your hands on your womb-space, if you like. (Goddess squat is a womb-honoring position. Like a Goddess statue, you want to be aligned so that your lifeline runs straight from the Earth up through your womb and out the top of your head.) You may hold this position for one or more breaths.
- Inhale up into Star pose. Hold this position for a breath or two.
- Exhale down into Triangle pose (the half-moon), turning the feet as shown.
- Inhale back to Star, then exhale down into Triangle on the other side.
- Inhale back through Star to Goddess. Hold as long as you like.
- Inhale up to Star again. Exhale.
- Step into Temple position as you inhale.
- Exhale down into a crescent moon on the left.
- Inhale up through Temple and exhale down into a crescent moon on the right.
- Return to Temple on the next inhalation.
- As you exhale, trace the full moon by circling your arms back down and around to Prayer pose (Namaste), with the palms pressed together in front of your heartspace.
- Bow, honoring the mother-to-be and Mother Earth.

Repeat the above series three or more times. You may need to talk the group through the first repetition, but by the second repetition or so, you will probably find that everyone follows along together quite smoothly without any verbal guidance. Stay tuned to the needs of your particular group and direct them only as much as necessary.

A group bellydance is another spiritually uplifting way of celebrating and honoring womanhood through the movement of your bodies. Or, provide hula skirts or silk scarves and some wild music to encourage uninhibited creative dance expression.

> To have everybody in the room moving in the same way was magical. I was surprised how quickly everyone got in sync, even the women there who would never go to a yoga class or get up and dance at a party. Everybody eased right into it. It was just magical.   — Barbara

Walkabout

The Walkabout, a Guatemalan ritual practiced by Quiché women seven months into pregnancy, is described by Deborah Jackson in *With Child* as being an intimate bonding time for the mother and her baby. She strolls along by herself, describing aloud to the baby inside all the familiar natural landmarks she encounters. A Walkabout could also take place within the home, with the mother telling the baby about the spaces and the special memories they evoke of people and pets in the family.

You may send the mother on a Walkabout walk in the half-hour or so before her Blessingway, especially if the ceremony will be taking place in her own home. Alternatively, incorporate a Walkabout into the Blessingway ceremony itself by walking en masse with the mother as she acquaints her baby with the world around her. Or, consider a people-oriented Walkabout, with the mother formally introducing the baby to each person present at her Blessingway.

Breaking Bread Together

Libations

A libation is the ritual pouring out of a drink as a prayerful act. Words of offering or appreciation are usually recited as a libation is poured, such as this prayer shared by Janice Robinson in *Pride and Joy*:

> "We ask God's blessing here today as we offer this sacrifice of thanks to our Creator. I pour this libation to ask that our...ancestors join us from the East [*pour the liquid on the ground in the direction of the East, then continue accordingly as you recite*], from the West, from the North, and from the South. With God in the forefront, our ancestors standing strong behind us, and our families beside us, there is nothing we cannot accomplish. Amen."

Any symbolic, personalized, or beautiful vessel may be used to hold a libation, and the liquid can be poured onto the Earth or into a bowl, gourd, or other receptacle such as a potted plant.

Water and wine are two liquids commonly used around the world for libations. Water, as the ultimate lifesource, is ripe with significance. Wine (especially red wine) represents our lifeblood and sometimes holds religious meaning as well. Cranberry juice and plum juice are excellent alternatives to wine; they have a similar mix of sweetness and bitterness to represent the joy and pain of childbirth. As Robinson says, "a traditional African libation of milk represents family, kindness, and acceptance. Milk libations are given as thanks for anything associated with the family or relatives..."

Hot tea can also be served ceremonially. Raven Lang suggests brewing a tea with herbs chosen to represent particular qualities with which you hope the pregnant mother will be blessed during her labor. For example, she mentions eyebright for clarity, squawvine for strength, lady slipper for endurance, black haw for peace of heart, and mother of the meadow for honoring the goddess. In "Blessingway," Gail Grenier Sweet suggests chamomile for relaxation, comfrey for healing, raspberry leaves to strengthen the uterus, and honey to represent sweetness. Or, simply choose herbs you know the honoree likes.

For the hot tea ritual, the midwife or the mistress of ceremonies serves tea to everyone in the circle, with the pregnant mother typically being served last. Each woman can extend her left palm cradled in her right palm, and receive a bit of tea that is just hot enough to hurt but not to burn. She can then drink the handful of tea. Or, each woman can touch her forehead to the tea, taste a bit with her tongue, and pour the rest over her head. Lang explains that "this signifies sharing and dispersing of the pregnant woman's pain in labor." The hot tea ritual fulfills a complexity of needs; the sister-circle symbolically bears the struggles of childbirth with the mother, while at the same time symbolically sharing its nourishment and gifts with her.

Drinking together is a universal way of celebrating special occasions and rites of passage. In Scotland, it is a time-honored practice for everyone to sip a libation from a communal cup in honor of the pregnant mother, says Connie Banack in "Blessing Way

Ceremonies: A Celebration." The passing around of a single cup ensures a ceremonial pace. You could also pour individual cups and toast the mother; in that case, I suggest using miniature cups so that the emphasis is not on the drink but rather on the act of sharing the ritual. Or, the mother-to-be may choose to pour the drinks herself, perhaps offering a blessing or appreciation to each woman she serves. This gives her an opportunity to do some giving and nurturing of others, bringing the Blessingway ceremony full circle.

Blossoming

Birth and blossoming flowers readily evoke images of one another. Blossoming rituals are a poetic way to acknowledge the budding of new life and a new identity for the pregnant woman.

Many foods can symbolize blossoming. A menu can be planned around such cycle-of-life foods as berries, watermelon, pomegranates, eggs, nuts, seeds, beans, edible flowers, and red wine or fruit juice. Red represents feminine power, so consider featuring it in your menu.

You may feed the mother a sample of each of the foods, perhaps speaking about what they symbolize as she tastes them. Or, recite a blessing as you present each food. For example, in *A Ceremonies Sampler*, Elizabeth Resnick Levine shares this biblically inspired sequence of blossoming foods and blessings:

> Now we partake of symbolic foods and participate in feeding
> [name]:
> Red wine for joyous celebration.
> *We bless the Source of Life, who has given us the sweet red fruit of the vine.*
> Round challah with raisins for sweetness and rising — a
> gradual growing, and the feminine shape of blossoming
> fertility.
> *We bless the Source of Life which creates bread from the Earth*

as she creates the power of life within us.
Raspberries, strawberries, watermelon, and other red fruits for
ripening, for blossoming, for beauty and femininity, for future
fruitfulness, and for the variety of experiences that await you.
*We bless the Source of Life that causes us to experience our
feminine beauty. We bless the Source of Life that enables us, like
the fruit, to ripen.*

Another blossoming ritual is a floral twist on libations. Everyone can bring a clean
flower that expresses her appreciation of the honoree. Drop the flowers into a water
bowl, then take turns drinking the flower essence water. Fertility, growth and change,
beauty, and new life are symbolized by the flowers themselves; the sharing of the
flower water signifies your solidarity behind the mother as she enters this new phase
of her life.

Feasts

The unifying power of breaking bread together is universally understood. From
Scotland to Indonesia, feasting has always been an integral part of celebrations.
Sharing a meal with others causes our bodies to release oxytocin, the "love hormone"
— the very same hormone that is involved in creating, birthing, feeding, and bonding
with a baby. It seems fitting, then, to feast together in celebration of the love that
brings a baby into the world and sustains him.

A feast is an opportunity for people to be holistically nourished by the Blessingway
experience. A potluck can also provide a way for each participant to contribute to the
nourishment of the new mother, the baby, and the group.

Feast foods are often symbolic, such as risen bread to represent life and fertility or
a cornucopia of fruits and nuts to represent abundant goodness (see **Blossoming**,
page 130, for more examples). The drawings below show a traditional Swedish circle
bread designed for sharing and a Greek brioche with a red-dyed egg in the middle,
symbolizing feminine power.

Illustration by Amanda Smith

To make breads like these, use a basic brioche recipe. For the Greek loaf, once the dough has risen, make a double-strand braid and bring the ends together to form a circle, then place it on a baking sheet with a dyed egg in the center. For the Swedish loaf, begin with the same double-strand braided circle, then surround it with roll-sized spiral twists of dough; when the dough rises again, they will join together.

Photo from Stephanie Peltier

Feast foods can be wildly festive or expressive, like the cake above. Cindy Parker describes her symbolic approach to a cake in "The Blessingway":"I like to serve a placenta cake for dessert. Simply make a round cake — spice, carrot, chocolate, whatever. Ice it with pink frosting and decorate it like a tree of life. Braid three red strings of licorice together to symbolize the cord. This is placed around the edge of the cake, then brought up the center to form the base of the tree. Other pieces of licorice may be added to make branches. I then decorate it with edible leaves and flowers."

Honey Cake
from *The Farm Cookbook*, reprinted with permission

I cup honey
1/4 cup water
2 cups rye flour
1 tsp. cinnamon
1/2 tsp. allspice
1/4 tsp. mace
2 t. baking powder
1/2 cup chopped nuts

Blend in honey and water, then beat in dry ingredients and blend in nuts. Pour into one 9" cake pan. Bake at 350 degrees with a pan of boiling water on the bottom of the oven for about 40 minutes. Let the cake age in plastic or a tin box for a few days before eating.

Everybody loves this cake. I made a little honey cake for my daughter for her first birthday, but for her cousins (who aren't used to "health foods") I bought a big storebought frosted cake. I couldn't believe it, though — they all ignored the one from Kroger and ate up every last bit of the honey cake instead.

— Stephanie

At my Blessingway, a fruit salad was presented in the form of a baby buggy carved out of a watermelon rind, with grapefruit rings for wheels. Simple ideas like this can transform everyday foods into fancy feast fare.

Illustration by Amanda Smith

Sometimes taking the time to savor just one special food together can be a delectable experience. The attachmentscatalog.com website described a Blessingway where one chocolate bon-bon per person was laid out on a silver platter. As everyone slowly and pleasurably tasted their bon-bons, they expressed their enjoyment through humming or whispering descriptions of the flavor. What a beautiful way to slow down and relish being together at the Blessingway; and what a nice reminder to similarly treasure each moment of pregnancy and parenting.

Whatever you serve, whether it is a single item, an extensive prepared menu, or a potluck, consider freezing some portion for the new parents to eat after the baby is born. Then they can defrost a helping of love whenever they need it!

A lot of the young women are mothers, that come to our Blessingways, and they're tired and they're up at night. And I would much rather that they take their time and energy to help the mother after the baby is born. So we had a rule, that they need to bring something to put on the food table that's really healthy but *that they didn't spend time preparing*, with the exception of one person who we designate to make something hearty for everybody. And that's a person who has the time, so there is always something there that's a warm casserole kind of thing.

— Nancy

The food is always healthy. There's never coffee. There's never caffeinated tea. We're feeding our bodies and our spirits and souls, so the food is always incredibly healthy and very beautiful.

— Marsha

Breaking the bread, eating and drinking together, felt more like communion after the emotions that came out during the Blessingway and the love that was generated. It had a real sense of ritual to it.

— Sandy

Reaching Out

Meal Trains

Around the world, women from many cultures share the tradition of doing all of the cooking — and often other chores as well — for the first thirty to forty days after the birth of a baby. This allows the mother, father and older siblings the freedom to rest, adjust to having a new baby in the home, and focus their time and attention on cherishing and bonding with the baby.

A meal train is a collaborative effort to ensure that the new parents are provided with nourishing meals for a period of time after the birth. When people call to RSVP, you can ask them to extend the sense of community spirit beyond the Blessingway itself by bringing a meal after the birth of the baby. Be sure to present the idea in a manner that allows people to decline graciously. Because of location, schedule, and other considerations, not everyone on the guest list will wish to participate. But for those who are willing and able, let them know that you will call to confirm the schedule of meals once the baby is born.

Alternatively, set out a signup sheet on the day of the Blessingway, with an explanation of the meal plan, the reasons behind it, and the logistics. A drawback to this approach is that some women may be too distracted during the Blessingway to notice the signup sheet, so it might be helpful to designate one person who can unobtrusively direct people's attention to it. Follow up with a phone call if you are unsure of anyone's intentions. Also call those who were unable to attend the celebration to offer them this opportunity to participate.

However you choose to organize it, if you are planning to provide meals, it is important to consult with the new mother about the specific needs of her family. Assess, for example, when she would find meals most helpful — beginning the day of the birth? After her mother leaves town? Daily? Every other day? You also need to know about any dietary restrictions or food preferences in her family, such as allergies, a vegetarian diet, or religious guidelines.

In order to be as helpful as possible, you may need to give specific guidance to the participants, such as suggesting that each person limit her mealtime visit to less than one hour, proposing that each of you do one chore of the mother's choosing while you are there, or offering the new parents the option of putting a cooler out on the front porch as a meal receptacle if they are not feeling up to receiving visitors that evening.

> We like to assure the new-mother-to-be that she will have two weeks of help. This is a major function of the Blessingway — to mobilize the woman's friendship circle at her time of greatest need. Our presence at the ceremony is our spiritual support, but this tangible, physical support rendered after the birth is just as important!
> — Nan Koehler, personal correspondence

The energy is so wonderful and it's so high and it's so delicious at the Blessingway itself that we have a sign-up sheet...to make sure that there is help for the mother for many weeks after the baby is born. And it's not just casseroles...it's laundry, it's coupons for things...That extends the loving and caring. And then you know when you have a baby someone may do that for you. It's just extending the family, because we don't have extended families here.

— Nancy

Long-Distance Blessingways

Sometimes it is impossible for friends and family to get together with an expectant or new mother. Many creative women have still found ways to convey their love and support by creating a long-distance Blessingway. Of course, without being physically together, certain ceremonial options — such as hairbrushing — are precluded. However, with a little imagination, a beautiful celebration can be crafted from afar. For a woman whose support circle is miles away, the value of such a gift can be immeasurable.

One aunt, whose pregnant niece was studying abroad, gathered all of her relatives and videotaped a ceremony in her honor. They sang special songs to her, then each in turn lit a candle and presented a symbolic gift. They boxed up the gifts and shipped them to her along with the videotape.

A woman whose pregnant friend had recently moved cross-country organized a special one-hour online chat room for friends and family to join together at an appointed time, taking turns sharing poems and readings and expressing their wishes for the new baby and her parents. (America Online lets members set up free private chat rooms or groups that allow access to anyone on the guest list, including non-AOL-members; other internet service providers may offer a similar service.)

Another woman crafted a keepsake album for a far-away new mother by asking each close friend and relative to contribute a written or typed copy of an inspirational reading about motherhood. Some people included accompanying artwork or photos.

A card shower can also bring hearts together from afar. It involves sending cards simultaneously to the honoree, so she receives them all at approximately the same time. To organize a card shower, extend a written invitation to everyone in her circle of friends and family, specifying the occasion or person(s) being honored or celebrated; your reason(s) for a card shower instead of an in-person gathering; the time frame within which all cards should be postmarked to create a shower effect; and the complete name and address of the recipient. You may also wish to give other explicit guidance such as requesting that each person enclose a bead so the recipient can string her own "birthing power" necklace, or encouraging handmade cards and/or handwritten sentiments in commercial cards. The card shower is a simple, long-lasting, and affordable way to surprise the mother-to-be with an outpouring of love, good wishes, and support.

After the Baby is Born

Childbirth is a brief event in a long process of life-change. It may be the peak of the transitional childbearing year, but it is not the only part of it that can be marked with a special ceremony. There are many reasons why it might be preferable to celebrate after the baby's birth. For instance, adoption and premature birth are specific circumstances that might call for an after-the-baby-comes ceremony. In some traditions, it is considered taboo to discuss or prepare for a baby before he is born. And nothing precludes having a mother-blessing or baby-welcoming ceremony after a baby is born, even if there was a Blessingway beforehand as well.

Many families have cultural or religious traditions to draw upon for welcoming a baby, such as the well-known Jewish traditions of naming ceremonies and brisses or the common Christian ritual of baptism. But for various reasons, even some religious families may choose to forego these traditional ceremonies; for example, with the medical evidence so solidly unsupportive of circumcision, many Jews are seeking alternatives to brisses. A Blessingway after the baby is born can give these families another way to celebrate the miracle of birth, honor the life-giving force of the woman, and consecrate both the bond between family members and their shared connection to their God.

The focus of a Blessingway after the baby comes might be on pampering the mother and valuing her for the work of bringing her baby into the world; giving the new mother and father courage for the challenges of parenting; saying "goodbye" to the before-baby woman and family and "hello" to their new incarnations; and/or welcoming the baby into the loving circle of your community.

One simple baby-welcoming ceremony that many midwives perform is a ritual bath, with the baby and possibly his mother, father, and/or older sibling(s) being given a soothing, healing herbal bath while songs of welcome or blessing are sung. Each person is then wrapped in a special towel or robe and put to bed, or pampered in other ways.

Other ceremonies for mothers and babies can easily be created, incorporating many of the rituals described in previous chapters.

Herbal Bath for Mother and Baby
(Courtesy of a local midwife)

The benefits of the herbal bath are threefold. First, it offers a warm, soothing environment for mother and baby to relax and enjoy getting to know one another. Second, the particular herbs are beneficial to the mom's perineal healing and prevention of infection. Third, the herbal bath offers a healthy and gentle alternative to conventional cord care for baby.

For a week's supply of herbal bath, you will need a minimum of the following:

⚘ 7 cups sea salt (antiseptic)
⚘ 3 cups uva ursi (antiseptic)

- 3 cups comfrey leaf (aids tissue healing)
- 3 cups shepherd's purse (reduces bleeding and swelling)
- 3 cups lavender flowers (antiseptic/aids tissue healing)
- 3 cups calendula flowers can be added for hemorrhoids or other varicosities.
- If you like the smell, you can add 4 - 6 bulbs of fresh garlic for extra prevention of infection, or as a substitute for the lavender.

These ingredients are all available by mail from the Blessed Herbs catalog (800-489-4372).

Directions:
In a large pot, bring 2 quarts water to a boil. Turn off heat and add a generous handful of each herb and a cup of sea salt. If you are using garlic, peel 4 to 6 cloves and cut into quarters, then add. Cover the pot and allow to steep for a minimum of one hour. (This mixture will keep up to 24 hours on the stove or longer in the fridge.) When ready, pour through a fine strainer or cheesecloth directly into a warm, hip-deep bath. The mother can sit and relax in the bath for a few minutes, then have someone hand the baby to her. She should hold the baby under the back of his head, facing her, allowing for free movement of arms and legs and submersion of the umbilical cord for rapid healing. Most babies really enjoy the water as long as their bodies are kept submerged for warmth. Usually if the baby cries during the bath it is because he is getting cold.

I usually give my clients a brief ceremony two weeks after the birth. I use Tibetan prayer bells or cymbals or fairy bells, to ground us. It makes everybody instantly be quiet and centered. Then I light a candle and I say a prayer to Grandfather Fire, the source of life. Then I say, "We are gathered here to give thanks for the safe passage of this baby and to focus once again on welcoming him."

The whole point of this ceremony is to get the people to realize that their baby isn't their object, that they have a responsibility to care for the baby and that the baby belongs to all of us, that we are all just part of the flow of life. So I smudge everybody to purify them, and I sing this song to everybody in the circle, close to their face: "We all come from God, and unto God we shall return. Like a ray of light, returning to the sun. Like a drop of water, flowing to the sea."

Then I put the baby on the ground. The Indian people would prepare a special place on a bed of sand, and they do it in the daylight, ideally when the sun is shining. Anyway, I put the baby naked on the ground, or whatever the people are comfortable with — on a receiving blanket, or if the baby is crying and really uncomfortable, the baby might nurse. And I say a prayer. It's a Navajo prayer that is done for the baby at this time, at two weeks.

I always get on my knees and I shake a rattle right at baby, and I say, "Ho, Earth. See me, I'm on my knees to you. I'm praying for this baby here. Make space for the baby, please, help the baby so that he may cross the

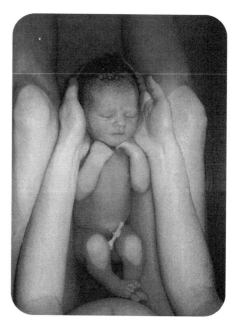

Photo by Merilynne Rush/John Bartholomew

brow of the first hill. Ho, grass, green things, plants that grow, see me, I'm on my knees to you. I'm praying for this baby here. Make space for the baby, please, help the baby so that he can cross the brow of the second hill. Ho, birds of the air, winged ones, see us here in this circle, see me, I'm on my knees to you. I'm praying for this baby here. Make space for the baby, please, help the baby so that he can cross the brow of the third hill. Ho, animals, four-leggeds, cats and dogs, things that creep and crawl, hear my voice, see me, I'm on my knees to you. I'm praying for this baby here. Make space for the baby, please, help the baby so that he can cross the brow of the fourth hill. Ho, rocks, things of the earth, plants that grow, winged ones in the sky, animals that creep and crawl, hear me, I'm praying for this baby here. Make space for the baby, please, help the baby so that he can cross the brow of many hills. Great spirits, help us to *follow* this baby into the new age." I always emphasize that we ar following this child into the future; this is our future lying on the sand bed here. And then I end with, "Thank you for the baby's safe passage. Mother Earth, Father Sky, thank you for our lives." — Nan Koehler

Sample Ceremonies

In quiltmaking, it is always a big thrill when all the pieces are finally stitched together into a cohesive whole. Similarly, the creative impact of a complete Blessingway ceremony is much greater than you might imagine when contemplating each separate part of it. So here are some samples of Blessingway "quilts" — ceremonies that American women have created. I hope this gives you an idea of the scope of possibilities.

A Blessingway in Margo's Honor

Introductions:

Everyone will have a turn to:
* Ring the bell,
* Tell us who you are and how you know Margo,
* Share what you appreciate most about Margo,
* Ring the bell again, then pass it on.

Presentation of the Group's Gift:

* We offer Margo something for her head — A tape recording of Barbara Kingsolver's novel, Animal Dreams
* We offer Margo something for her hands — a skein of rainbow yarn and some circular needles, so she can knit those baby hats she keeps talking about making
* We offer Margo something for her heart — A necklace of intertwined hearts (handcrafted by Jenna)
* We offer Margo something for her health and the baby's health — Apricot massage oil, and a gift certificate for a postpartum massage and infant massage class with SueEllen's aunt Jean

Singalong:

Those of us who play instruments brought them, the rest of us have songs to share. So let's all raise our voices together in song for Margo.

Potluck feast:

And cake! (Baked with love by Margo's mom, Leanne)

Welcome to Gabrielle's Blessingway

We gather together today to honor our sister Gabrielle, to offer her our blessings, and help light the way for her journey. She has been a warm giving spirit to the world, and today we will honor her pregnancy with a Blessing Way Ceremony.

We prepare and form a sacred circle for Gabrielle to relax and enjoy her Blessings. The sacred circle surrounds and protects her as the sacred circle of her womb surrounds and protects her unborn child.

Each of us find a place in the circle, and place a candle in front of us. The Smudge bowl is then passed to purify. As you breathe the aromatic herbs, remember that you are in a sacred space, in a timeless moment of ritual.

The yarn will be woven between us, and later used to create the bracelets that we wear until Gabrielle gives birth. This signifies our connection to Gabrielle.

We will start by helping Gabrielle get comfortable. We will then start the Blessings. We begin from the right, light our candle with Gabrielle's candle, and offer our Blessing, gift, poem or words of significance. These candles become Gabrielle's to light her way for her birth, where they will all be burned together. After the Blessings, the grooming will begin. Once the ceremony has been completed, and we have our bracelets to connect us all to Gabrielle, we will share lunch, and socialize.

Thank you for sharing in this blessed event.

We call upon the five sacred elements as we bless Tina today.

Air: sweetgrass smudge
Water: footwashing
Earth: hairbrushing and floral headwreath
Fire: Candlelighting
Spirit: songs of blessing

Blessed be!

For Marcy

We start by honoring the women who mothered us and our place in the line of mothers before us. We honor the timelessness of the work of birth and of motherhood.

Naming: I am Donna, granddaughter of Nellie and Doris, daughter of Ellen, mother of Adam.

We encourage Marcy as she gives voice to her hopes and dreams for this labor and this baby.

Light candle: Marcy to speak her hopes/wishes. We add our own voices in wishing well for Marcy and Ian's baby. Each woman to speak/write her wishes for Marcy and for Chuckles.

We support Marcy as she gives voice to her fears. For once fears are spoken, though they remain, they lose some power over us. Marcy, blow out the candle. As the smoke dissipates, so may your fears let go of you and leave you stronger.

We offer physical support and affection through the washing of feet.

We acknowledge the importance of humor and wisdom in family life. Marcy's mother, who was unable to be here, has started the stories. I read for her.

Share stories. Begin by reading Sue's.

We break bread together to nourish the body, the baby and the soul.

Welcome to Arianne's Blessingway. Here is how I envision things flowing, but if the spirit moves you, feel free to add other elements to the ceremony.

Centering the energy: Guided meditation (holding hands)

Raising the energy: chanting, drumming

Directing the energy: hairbrushing with storytelling, "circle of love" ritual

Grounding the energy: moment of silence, feast, sign up to bring meals after the baby is born

---

Welcome to Carol's Blessingway! Please take off your shoes, then join the circle silently. When everyone is present, Martha will lead us in prayer.

Then, Carol will introduce everyone and tell us about her special connection with each person. After that, we will have an opportunity to present her with our gifts to open.

Finally, we will each light a candle on the cake and say a few words of inspiration or encouragement before we sing Happy Birthday to Carol and the baby, hug, and eat!

Blessingway for Shelly Emmett

Opening Poem
Blessed Be my brain
that I may conceive of my own power.
Blessed Be my breast
that I may give sustenance to those I love.
Blessed Be my womb
that I may create what I choose to create.
Blessed Be my knees
that I may bend so as not to break.
Blessed Be my feet
that I may walk in the path of my highest will.
— Robin Morgan

Opening Song
From a Woman we were born into this circle; From a Woman we were born into this world (sing 4x's)

Introductions
Maternal line of lineage

True Home Ritual
Silently lead your guests through your home. Circle an incense stick
above your head and let the scented smoke waft into the four
corners of each room. Say together:
Bless all who live here —
ones held most dear:
From corner to corner
and pillar to post,
Cleanse this house and
protect to the utmost.
So mote it be,
one, two, three.

Footbath for Shelly
Given to her by her mother

Belly Painting and Toe Nail Painting
To celebrate Shelly and her beautiful, growing body.

Sharing of Words and Beads
These will provide comfort to Shelly as she labors
and will one day show the baby that he or she
was loved even before birth.

Lighting of Candles
and Egg Ceremony
Sitting in a circle, pass an egg around the circle to represent the continuity of life. As you pass your egg, light your candle to represent the light of this life that is about to be born. As Shelly labors, you will be called and asked to light your candle again so Shelly can focus on the energy from this day and have it help her in her journey to bring this new life into our circle.

Lunch
Pomegranate Salad with Almonds and Cheese
Pomegranates were symbolic of birth and fertility in many cultures. The word pomegranate means "apple with many seeds." The fruit, with its red juice and numerous offspring, was almost universally known as a womb symbol. The almond has ancient roots as a birth and fertility symbol because of its similarity in shape to the female genitals and was once a sign of virgin motherhood. Cheese has long been associated with the mysteries of birth and lactation. The Egyptians pictured the human body as a product of mother's milk "curdled" into solid matter as the child grew and put on new flesh.

Round, Sweet Bread
Naked Pregnant Shelly Cake
Strawberry Moon Tea

Blessingway
for Gloria Stone
April 29, 2001

Welcome! Welcome to this Blessingway celebration for Gloria! We gather here today as friends to participate in this rite of passage. The Blessingway is a Navajo tradition used to bless the one sung over to ensure good luck, good health and blessings. This Blessingway ceremony ritualizes our support of Gloria. By being in this sacred circle of Blessingway, we also confirm our connection with all living beings.

In the center of our circle, we have a symbol for each of the five elements to create balanced energy:

- For earth, a crystal
- For water, floating flowers
- For fire, a candle
- For air, incense
- For ether, a conch shell

To begin our ceremony, we will cast our sacred circle by passing this incense round the circle to purify our space. Since this is a Navajo tradition, we will play a Native American song to ground us for this ceremony.

Casting the Circle — Introductory Song

Where I Sit is Holy

Where I sit is holy; holy is the ground
Forest, mountain, river; listen to the sound
Great Spirit circles all around me

Who I am is holy; holy are we
Body, thought, emotion, connecting you and me
Great Spirit circles all around me

What I do is holy; holy is my way
Work and play together, celebrate the day
Great Spirit circles all around me

We are here to honor Gloria who will be a mother. As she makes the passage through pregnancy and labor, her life will change forever. She takes on the care of another life with her own. We are here today to invoke the spirit of the Goddess in wishing Gloria a safe birth, a strong child and happiness in motherhood.

Connection: To begin our ceremony, let's go around the circle and have each person introduce yourself and describe your connection to Gloria. Describe how you met, what drew you to her and why she is important to you.

Birthing Necklace: In Africa, the midwives bring a birthing necklace to each delivery. The necklace symbolizes our shared experience as women. The birthing necklace provides focus and is a calming influence as women hold it during labor. After each delivery, the woman adds her own bead to the necklace.

Today, we will make a birthing necklace for Gloria. I will pass around this bowl of beautiful glass beads. As the bowl is passed to you, select a bead. We will pass a silk thread around the circle. Each woman will place her bead on the silk and share her own stories of birth, positive advice, and/or stories about what children have meant in their lives.

Poem:

The Faith Poem, by Patrick Overton

Blessings: We have come to share our blessings for Gloria and her baby, John Lawrence Stone. I will pass around this candle. Beneath the candle, there is an ultrasound picture of baby John to help provide connection to this new life.

Each woman shares blessings.

Group: Gloria, the sacred journey of motherhood is before you and within you. We celebrate today to honor your body and the new life you hold. We bless every part of you. You symbolize before us the process of creation and the miracle of birth that belongs uniquely to women. Feel the love and support of this community of women.

Cradling: In many ways, motherhood is the ultimate sacrifice – the laying down your life for the sake of another. We want Gloria to feel precious, cared for and loved so this feeling can sustain her in the challenging times, so we, her friends will cradle her!

Women stand in two rows facing each other and hold wrists to form a cradle. One woman supports head and another supports feet. Gloria lays back onto cradle and is lifted and rocked gently. Music: Lifted Up By Angels (from Christine Dente's album: Along the Road).

Closing: Gloria, may your journey be empowering and affirming. When you reach difficult points, know that the strength of eons of foremothers flows in your veins and call upon the power and love of your friends here around you today. We are with you in our hearts. Blessed be!

VARIATIONS ON THE PATTERN: BLESSINGWAYS FOR OTHER TRANSITIONS

Adoption

Adopting a child is a unique transition for the mother, the father, and any other children in the family. Because they are going through every step of this transformational experience together, consider including the father and other children in the Blessingway. On the other hand, it may still make perfect sense to keep the ceremony focused on just the mother, in the time-honored way of women gathering ceremonially to welcome, guide and support another woman as she enters the realm of new motherhood.

In a Blessingway for adoption, you will celebrate life and love, perhaps focusing on the rewards of parenthood, the fact that this child will be greatly cherished, and the strength that the mother and father will need to parent this child. It is wonderful to honor the birth mother in some small way as well, even if you do not know her name.

Simply mentioning her may be enough, or recognize her more formally by lighting a candle for her or offering a libation in her honor.

A symbol for adoptive families is a heart with a triangle in its center. This represents the birth family, the adoptive family, the child, and their loving union. You might include this symbol somehow — perhaps on the invitations, on a printed program, or as a cake decoration. My sister combined it with other symbols on the invitation below; she explains that she chose "sunrise/sunsets in the front wings for life's cycles, hearts in the abdomen for love and family connections, leaves in the hind wings for growth and life, a yin-yang symbol for the complement of feminine and masculine, and the butterfly itself for change, transformation, beauty, and journeys."

Since adoption entails a physical and emotional journey for all involved, an Arch ritual may make sense as a symbolic way to show the family that your love and support will travel with them every step of the way.

Or give the adoptive parents pre-stamped, pre-addressed postcards, with a space for them to write in the date they will be bringing their son or daughter home. When they leave to pick up their child, they can mail the postcards to friends and family. It will be encouraging for them to know that their loved ones will be thinking of them as they make that special journey.

A Blessingway is significant for any woman about to achieve a child. I found it extremely appropriate for adoption, which is not the traditional or usual way to have a child, although I'm sure adoption has been around since the beginning of time. A Blessingway is not only a beautiful way to recognize the acquisition of a child, but it's also a healing ceremony to say "we recognize you as 100% woman even if your ovaries aren't functioning or even if your womb is not present. You're still 100% woman and 100% mother."

— Barbara

People were recognizing and honoring our struggle to conceive and give birth to this child in such a different way, through lots of paperwork and traveling and waiting, which is labor but it's a very different kind of labor.

A Blessingway Ceremony

Honoring Barbara Harvey
~ as a woman and a mother

Come celebrate with Barbara as she, Bill and Morgan prepare to bring home their new baby boy!

We will gather at Barbara's house, 1297 Newport Rd. promptly at 4:00 p.m. on Saturday, December 2nd

Please bring:
- A short poem, reading or song about motherhood
- 1-4 beads for a necklace we will make together for Barbara
- A small token symbolic of your love, blessings or wishes for Barbara and/or baby

RSVP (yes or no) by Thanksgiving ~ call Shari Maser at 734-426-1641.

~ Hors D'oeuvres will be served.

~ Lap babies welcome.

Barbara's Blessingway:
Ceremonial Progression

❧ **Friendship arch**

with song: *Child of Mine*

Child of mine, blessed one,
your journey has been long but you're almost home.

❧ **Hairbrushing**

❧ **Introductions and Appreciations**

❧ **Moon Salutations**

❧ **"The Tie that Binds" and Presentations:**

Light a candle...add a flower...make an altar contribution...share your reading...
add a bead to the necklace...wrap the yarn around your wrist

with song between presentations: *Love Grows* (refrain) by Tom Pease

Love grows, one by one
two by two, and four by four
Love grows round like a circle
and comes back knocking on your front door.

❧ **Group hug**

with closing song: *It's in Every One of Us* by David Pomeranz

It's in every one of us to be wise.
Find your heart, open up all your eyes.
We can love everything
without ever knowing why.
It's in every one of us, you and I.

Giving us a send-off for "wow, look what you've been through" and "here are our well wishes as your baby comes home" was very meaningful to me.

— Marlene

That day for me was really beautiful. One thing that made it exceptional is that it was the day before we were to leave on our transatlantic flight. I felt like I was sailing on the wings that these women sent us on.

— Barbara

Having my Blessingway at my own house was really special. All that energy that was created stayed in the house, because what I did was I left the altar sitting there for the whole time we were gone. It was so comforting to think about that while we traveled to and from Russia.

— Jenny

Grieving and the Loss of a Baby

Pregnancy-related losses can occur under many circumstances, including miscarriage, stillbirth, abortion, giving a baby up for adoption, and SIDS. The juxtaposition of birth and death often makes these experiences exceptionally challenging to process. A Blessingway ceremony can ease the way by bringing an intimate group together to share the grief and the jumble of other emotions. The Blessingway offers a forum for honoring the pregnancy, the birth, the baby, the parents, and the divine; saying goodbye; and openly acknowledging the pain of the loss.

Veronica and Tom, whose first baby was stillborn, held a series of memorial ceremonies — two months after their daughter's birth and death, then several months later as an extension of the annual hospital-sponsored memorial service, and finally on the anniversary of their baby's death. These simple ceremonies demonstrate how the Blessingway concept can be adapted effectively for a loss.

Luna's Memorial Service, At Home
March 2002

- Candlelighting, with music
- Presentation of altar contributions
- Sharing our thoughts about Loss and Love, and what we learned from Luna
- Veronica reading from her pregnancy journal
- Writing wishes and regrets; burning them away
- Hold hands for a moment of silence
- Potluck, with music

Luna's Memorial Service, Outside the Hospital
September 2002

- Smudging with sage
- Candlelighting and display of Luna's photograph
- Veronica sings and plays the guitar for Luna
- Hold hands for a moment of silence

Luna's Remembrance
February 2003

- Stargazing
- Candlelighting
- Visit to the cemetery, decorating Luna's grave

What follows is an outline of another family's Blessingway, given upon the birth and subsequent death of their baby boy.

Purposes of this Blessingway memorial service
* Celebration of Philip joining our (extended) family
* The joy of his coming
* Commemoration of his time with us
* His passing again into the higher worlds

Opening
* "Censing" with smudge of sage
* A song to set the tone
* Weaving of the thread of life
  * Two poems

from "Twist Ye, Twine Ye" by Sir Walter Scott

Twist ye, twine ye! even so
Mingle shades of joy and woe
Hope and fear and peace and strife,
In the thread of human life.
Passions wild and follies vain,
Pleasures soon exchanged for pain;
Doubt and jealousy and fear,
In the magic dance appear.

Now they wax and now they dwindle,
Whirling with the whirling spindle,
Twist ye, twine ye! even so
Mingle human bliss and woe.

from "Auguries of Innocence" by William Blake

Joy and woe are woven fine,
A clothing for the soul divine;
Under every grief and pine
Runs a joy with silken twine.
It is right it should be so;
Man was made for joy and woe;
And when this we rightly know,
Thro' the world we safely go.

* Light a candle to signify his conception

Body of Ceremony
* Observations on the pregnancy
* The Rainbow Bridge legend
* Honey to celebrate the sweetness of his birth as story is told
* Remembrances of his birth
* Sharing of "gifts" by others relevant to having a new, unseen family member
* An offering from the heart, of a joyous nature — such as music, poetry, or flowers

Closing
* Hot tea to commemorate the sting of death
* Cutting the thread of life
* Extinguish the candle
* Song: "I am Walking in the Light"
* Postlude:
* Gifts from Philip
* Shared reflections on mysteries of birth and death

Philip's mother Monica encourages "making a lighting of candles part of the Blessingway, with one candle per person. Ask them to light their candles on anniversaries of the loss, perhaps daily at first, then weekly, then monthly. It could be a comfort to the mother to know that friends were taking the time to remember her and her baby at difficult times." Four herbs that Monica has used "in wreaths and to decorate candles to give to people after a loss are Rosemary for Remembrance, Sage to Mitigate Grief, Thyme for Courage, and Lavender to Soothe the Mind."

Dancing up the Moon by Robin Heerens Lysne tells the story of Jane, who was grieving a miscarriage. Her intimate ceremony included her mother and two friends, and was quite spontaneous. Under an oak tree in the backyard, they stood in a circle, holding onto a big bouquet of balloons. After taking "three deep breaths together to help us begin," Jane tearfully began to share her feelings. She expressed sadness "that I'm not pregnant," guilt "that I couldn't prevent this miscarriage," and love for her baby. With each statement, the other women repeated Jane's words back to her, then Jane used a beloved aunt's old hat pin to pop a balloon. She ended the ritual by saying, "I love you and bless you, little spirit. I hope you will try again when it's the right time." Finally, she released the last balloon into the air, and watched it disappear as her mother and her friends embraced her. This one little ritual had a big impact on Jane and on the women there with her.

Gathering with loving intentions and sharing a ritual can also contribute to the healing process in other situations in which a mother and father are grieving. For example, "Healing Abortion Ritual" in the Autumn 2002 issue of *The Mother Magazine* describes a healing ceremony designed to address the impact of an abortion on the mother, the father, and others.

In "Healing Cesarean Section Trauma: A Transformational Ritual," Jeannine Parvati Baker proposes a ceremony that can help a new mother cope with this particular kind of pregnancy-related grief, which so often goes unacknowledged in our culture. She suggests that the ceremony be a forum in which the new mother can meditate upon all that contributed to her baby being born by Cesarean section, offer forgiveness to herself and all those who were part of that process, express appreciation for the honor of being entrusted to care for a new life, and express gratitude for the lessons learned from the surgical birth.

In *Welcoming the Soul* of a Child, Jill Hopkins suggests that "if the purpose [of a ritual] is to heal a difficult or traumatic birth, state that in your opening prayers. Bring into the circle a symbol of the birth. Share your feelings and thoughts about the birth. What did this experience teach or heal?...After sharing your thoughts and feelings about the birth, wrap the symbol up in a piece of fabric. Either bury it under leaves or in the ground, or burn it. You can do this as part of the ritual now or later." To mark her loss of fertility after an emergency hysterectomy, a local young woman asked friends to join her in a similar ritual to help her come to terms with the unexpected reality that she would never birth a baby. This kind of healing ritual could also be modified for parents who have lost a baby.

Many of the rituals described in previous chapters could be adapted to mark a pregnancy-related loss as well. For example, the yarn of a Blessingway bracelet "can symbolize the thread of life being severed, or it could be the binding together in community," suggests Rahima Baldwin Dancy.

In addition to formal rituals, group hugs and the sharing of a meal can be cathartic. Your support can be further extended by making arrangements for ongoing help with chores and meals during the weeks or months following the loss.

Grieving is always a long process; but beyond that commonality, everyone's experience of grief is unique. Each person will have different needs at different times. Thus, when planning a Blessingway for a grieving family, it is essential to communicate extensively with them. Ask what they need with love in your heart, listen openly, attentively and intuitively, and then craft a ceremony that is responsive to their needs.

> After 7 weeks, I decided I was ready to do a memorial service. We decided to invite no family. In fact, we didn't tell our families about it because I felt like this service had to be for us. I remember wanting to just be with my friends and be supported. And I just felt even though some of my family was supportive, I wouldn't be able to get what I needed if it were about my family.
> — Veronica

I had everyone who was at her birth write me a letter as to what they learned from the experience. I just felt like I needed to have people tell me that her death happened for something worthwhile.   — Lynn

It was very fitting. There was a sense of taking the first step toward closure and of really honoring the baby, honoring the family and the change rather than "Boom. It's done. It's over. Let's not talk about it." Certainly a healing. It validates the experience, validates the being, validates that it happened. There's the grieving and it's a reality.
— Rahima

A lot of people came up to me and said that the service was really helpful for them — either because it was helpful for them to help us, or helpful for them because they felt some sense of loss as well. It was really healing for them too.   — Lynn

It was good for me to hear other people say that they loved and supported us. I remember one woman saying that she wanted us to know that she thought we were really amazing parents for loving our daughter the way that we did. I just remember that comment in particular was really helpful.   — Veronica

Perhaps a Blessingway for a New and Grieving Mother should be thought of in segments. One part is about the pregnancy and the birth and the baby (the new mother), and another part for the grieving mother (and father, if appropriate).   — Monica

It seems that a memorial service a short time after the birth and death (and for us 4 weeks was plenty soon enough) should be just that, a memorial service. What would have been incredible would have been a Blessingway for me at the time of his due date. (Until then, I could say to myself, "I should still be pregnant." At the due date, I realized, even more painfully, "I should have a baby now!") This scenario would ensure that the mother is not forgotten at one of the most difficult times, when most everybody is hoping and assuming that she's getting "back to normal..."

A Blessingway on the due date could have been focused on me. Perhaps at that point I could have thought clearly about what would be right and helpful for me, and could have invited only those people with whom I could be totally open, those who could handle my tears and pain.

— Monica

Other Occasions

The Blessingway concept is applicable beyond the childbearing year; it can be used to honor and support women and their families through a wide variety of rites of passage throughout their lives.

Meaningful ceremonies can be created for a baby's first birthday or other such milestones, the weaning of a nursing baby or toddler, the onset of menarche or menopause, high school or college graduations, weddings, anniversaries, birthdays, New Year's Eve celebrations, retirement, goodbyes, housewarmings, and healing before or after illness or surgery or divorce.

Ritual celebration of the milestones in a child's life can take many forms, just as Blessingways can. For example, in China it is traditional to celebrate a child's "first-moon" or one-month birthday. A Navajo tradition is called a Laughing Party; as explained to me by the mother of a Navajo boy, this is a ceremonial celebration of the emergence of the child's individual spirit. As the name suggests, the Laughing Party is made after the child begins to laugh; it is traditionally thrown by the first person who inspires the baby to laughter.

Another approach would be to celebrate the child's first birthday with a few special rituals instead of the usual cake and cookies. Perhaps you might choose Wishes for Baby (and/or advice for the parents), Quilts, or Gifts from the Heart (presenting heartfelt gifts for baby and/or his mother and father, since it is their "birth-day" too!). Singing and dancing are also fun to include.

It is wonderful to have a special way to collect the gifts or wishes bestowed upon the baby, so that when he is older, he can carry them or look at them whenever he likes. For this purpose, my sister used rose petals from her garden and feathers from her hens to decorate a homegrown gourd, then she filled the cavity with a few time-capsule-type mementos. Wendy, a Jewish friend of mine, made a button-up bag with a Tree of Life beaded onto it, and gave it to the baby's mother to fill with sacred items of her choosing. Other alternatives include a personalized box or scrapbook.

Jill Hopkins describes a ceremony for a toddler in *Welcoming the Soul of a Child*, "...I read a passage from Jack Kornfield's beautifully written book, A Path With Heart. He tells of a tribe of people in East Africa who recognize the birth date of a child prior to conception. For this tribe, the child is born the first time the child is a thought in its mother's mind. When she wishes to conceive a child, she goes out into the bush and sits alone under a tree. There she waits and listens until she hears the song of the child that she will give birth to. Conception occurs, in the eyes of these people, at the moment this song is heard. The mother then returns home and teaches the song to the father, so that while making love the child's spirit is called to them. The midwives and villagers are then taught the melody, so that during labor and the moment of birth itself the child is welcomed into this world with his or her own very special song. This same song is sung during childhood illnesses, personal celebrations, initiations, and rites of passage. And at the end of one's life, loved ones gather around the deathbed to sing this song for the very last time."

In Hopkins' soul-welcoming ceremony for a toddler, this story is shared aloud, then the mother sits by a tree and waits to hear her child's song. The child sings, dances, or speaks when ready. Then the mother returns to the larger group and teaches her partner the "song" of the child. They teach it to "midwives and elders" and other loved ones. They reenact the birth and welcome the child with his song once again. Thus the child is honored as a valued member of the family.

One grandmother created a ceremony to celebrate her granddaughter Melanie in her soon-to-be new role as a big sister. She planned a formal teaparty for a small group of girls, asking each to bring along something that would help Eliza be a loving big sister. The tea ritual symbolically demonstrated the importance of this transition for Eliza. The presentation of big-sister gifts gave Eliza's young friends a meaningful way to acknowledge the major change that was imminent in her life, and to be supportive of her.

My family has found that ritual can inspirit and enrich any special gathering. So when grandparents came to visit, we held the following ceremony in honor of my two daughters and their special relationship as sisters.

Sisters Ceremony

Illustration by Amanda Smith

(Note: Most of the text that follows is excerpted verbatim or adapted from Andrea Alban Gosline's beautiful book, *Welcoming Ways*. Gosline gives credit for inspiration to Anita Diamant's *The New Jewish Baby Book*.)

(*Ring bell*) Erica, you have just turned three. (*Count out three orange marbles*) And Alex, since you are her sister, here are three matching marbles for you. Alex, you are about to turn six (Count out six blue marbles) and Erica, since you are her sister, here are six matching marbles for you too. This feels like an extra special time, a time to be honored and appreciated because, for this one time in your lives, Erica will be exactly half Alex's age and Alex will be exactly double Erica's age. These marbles represent the magic of your connection to each other as sisters. (Give each a swirled marble)

Now we celebrate your life together as sisters.

I reawaken Alex and Erica's sense of sight with the light of these candles. (*Light candles*) Women have kindled the spiritual flame for home and family since ancient times. May our girls experience the warmth and caring of community and share their enlightenment with each other and everyone else they meet.

I reawaken Alex and Erica's sense of taste with this drop of sweet wine. (*Give taste on tongue*) Nature provides the fruit we transform into wine. We thank the Earth for this gift. May our girls be nourished by the abundance Nature gives us and take pleasure in her gifts.

I reawaken Alex and Erica's sense of sound with this bell. (Ring bell) Music encircles us with a symphony of celebration. May the sound of joy and love caress our girls' ears and fill their hearts.

I reawaken Alex and Erica's sense of smell with these flowers. (*Let each girl smell one, then place it in her hand to keep*) The sense of smell brings our awareness to the essence of life and reminds us of the soul. May the flowers' fragrance surround our girls and cultivate a joyful and generous spirit in each of them.

I reawaken Alex and Erica's sense of touch with this water. (*Wash their hands with it*) Water bathes us in truth and hope. May our girls immerse themselves in the sea of life and enjoy it together.

Song (*from* Barney)
I love you, you love me, we're a happy family
with a great big hug (*pass a hug around the circle*)
and a kiss from me to you (*pass a kiss around the circle*)
won't you say you love me too? (*say "I love you"*)

(*Hold hands in a circle*) As family, we have a special kind of love for each other. We affirm our connection with Alex and Erica with these promises:

(*Each person make a promise, such as:*
I will do my best to help Alex and Erica grow up.
I will do my best to share with Alex and Erica what I love about life.
I will do my best to be patient with Alex and Erica.)

(*Ring bell*) Behold our family here assembled. We are thankful for this place in which we dwell, for the love that unites us, for the peace accorded us this day, for the hope with which we expect tomorrow, for the health, the work, the food, and the bright skies that make our lives delightful, and for our family and friends in all parts of the earth. Give us courage and gaiety and quiet mind. (Ring bell)

This bread represents abundance and is a symbol of gratitude and reciprocity. May Alex and Erica always enjoy and appreciate the pleasures of sharing a meal with loved ones. (*Pass bread for all to eat*)

And now, Alex and Erica, as sisters, you may hold your swirled sister marbles in your hands and blow out the candles together. (Blow out candles; ring bell)

I was recently invited to a ceremony for a woman embarking upon a divorce from the father of her three young children. Her invitation, below, demonstrates another way the Blessingway concept can be applied creatively to any major life transition.

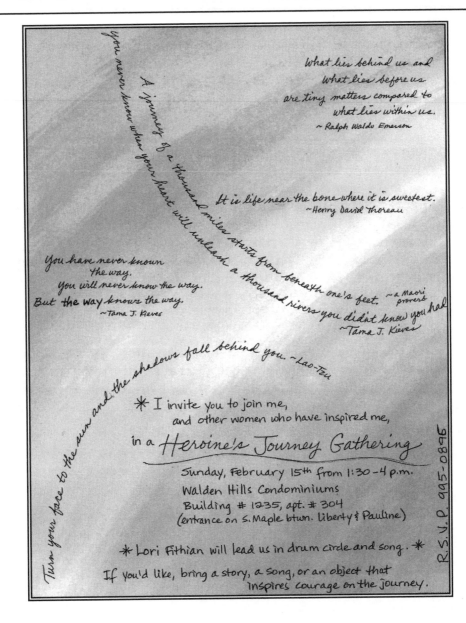

What lies behind us and
what lies before us
are tiny matters compared to
what lies within us.
~ Ralph Waldo Emerson

A journey of a thousand miles starts from beneath one's feet. ~ a Maori proverb

You never know where your heart will unleash a thousand rivers you didn't know you had ~Tama J. Kieves

It is life near the bone where it is sweetest.
~ Henry David Thoreau

You have never known
the way.
You will never know the way.
But the way knows the way.
~Tama J. Kieves

Turn your face to the sun and the shadows fall behind you. ~ Lao-Tzu

✳ I invite you to join me,
and other women who have inspired me,

in a *Heroine's Journey Gathering*

Sunday, February 15th from 1:30 – 4 p.m.
Walden Hills Condominiums
Building # 1235, apt. # 304
(entrance on S. Maple btwn. Liberty & Pauline)

✳ Lori Fithian will lead us in drum circle and song. ✳

If you'd like, bring a story, a song, or an object that
inspires courage on the journey.

R.S.V.P. 995-0896

A friend of mine got divorced and she called and said that she was having a ceremony for her divorce. When I went I realized that a Blessingway could be for any transition — filling up the person and loving them and having them walk out feeling filled with confidence and love and support and caring that could carry them through this event in their life.

— Nancy

My thirtieth birthday was a significant point in my life and I wanted some way to honor it. I expressed that to a friend and lamented that I didn't have many friends because I was new here, and I felt like I needed more support. So she planned a Blessingway for me. We started outside. She had cut off willow branches from the willow tree in her backyard and made a wreath for me. Then we sang some songs before moving inside for dessert and gifts. Every single gift was homemade and personal. I still have the socks Mary made me, and the poster Deb made for me. My Blessingway made me feel very special, at a time when I really needed that.

— Merilynne

I'm already thinking about times in my baby daughter's life when I'm imagining I'll want to do something ceremonial for her and with her. This Blessingway concept entered my life in the birth arena, but now it is going to be part of me forever.

— Robin

V

SCRAPS AND THREADS

Women Across North America Share Their Insights

Blessingway is...

The Blessingway is a time when her community of women can come together to pay homage, to honor her as a woman about to bring new life into the world. It's a very meaningful, spiritual kind of experience for everyone there. I think most people crave that kind of experience in their life.

— Kathi

It's about helping women to find their center, find their strength. It's a real grounding, centering kind of thing, and very life-affirming.

— Jennifer

A Blessingway gives you the chance to slow down, stop the rush of life, have some quiet, deep time together and celebrate a rite of passage.

— Amy

During birth and the years mothering her children, a woman will need to access her courage and power, gentleness and patience, over and over again. The Blessingway ceremony is a time when her loving community is present to remind her that she embodies these qualities always and can call upon them.

— Francine

I like the fact that a Blessingway is not so stuff-oriented, it's more person-centered.

— Gabrielle

The emphasis is to show honor, show love, show nurturance, to build a wall of protection around the birthing woman, to bind the woman's community together. It's also about recalling ancient times, when women held the mysteries.

— Lori

It's a way for the community to say, "Pay attention! This is important. This is a transition. This is out of the ordinary and we're coming together to mark this, to honor her and to wish her well." And I think that's what we're all looking for — how to feel the divine or the sacred in everyday life, how to take note of that, and how to create community.

— Rahima

It felt right to be the center of attention. After all, it was going to be my birth-day too! I really was going to be birthing both my son, and myself as his mother.

— Wendy

The nature of Blessingway — honoring women and women's bodies and women in their roles — speaks to me of the Goddess tradition, and I feel that that is somewhat lost in our society. I think women in our society have not been encouraged to get into groups and do powerful things so it's new to a lot of women. Women really looking into their core and finding power there is not something we've been taught to do, but this is one way we can do it. I think that's why I love Blessingways so much.

— Barbara

A Blessingway is about how you can do deliciously nurturing and honoring things to support a woman in preparation for this amazing thing that she is going to have happen.

— Bronwen

I think it's really what baby showers ought to be, or used to be — the community coming together to give her their blessing.

— Rahima

A Blessingway is about the mother and the birth process. We are going to weave a web of protection and love and honor and respect around this woman. We are not gathering to deal with the baby; this is all about the mother.

— Gae

The key is intention

Judith decided to give me a Blessingway because she really wanted to celebrate me as a woman and give me support, guide me through the transitions.

— Ann

The sacred mysteries of life deserve the awe, the exaltation, and the deliberate attention of a Blessingway ceremony.

— Amy

We felt intuitively that we should prepare for this rite of passage into parenthood with some kind of ceremony. It just seemed right. But neither of our religious or cultural traditions seemed to offer anything more than the typical buy-us-lots-of-stuff baby shower, so Dan and I decided to create our own ceremony with whatever rituals made sense to us.

— Sue

We tend to judge being "needy" as a critical thing, instead of finding a positive way to fulfill those needs, instead of saying, "it's OK to want attention… here it is, we love you, we'll give it to you." — Patty

The welcoming of labor, the welcoming of parenthood and motherhood, is much more the focus than actual gift-giving. — Melanie

The purpose of the Blessingway is to highlight the sharing of experiences and the presence of these other people who are there for you and the handing down of wisdom. And it's much more focused on the ritual than it is on any kind of gift-giving. People did bring gifts to my Blessingway, but it was peripheral. It was later on, after we had done the whole ritual and we all talked a bit, we had something to eat, and then the gifts were just incidental. — Michelle

I have been to Blessingways that occur spontaneously. You basically can create one right then and there and you don't have to boil water and you don't have to have any paraphernalia. You basically have the circle, and maybe you will light a candle and maybe you will ring a bell and the prayers will come and the holding will come or the tears will come. And at the end of whatever happens, the person realizes, "Today has been transformational. I can go back to the hospital and face the rest of this journey. I have been given this strength. I have been given a new insight." And this is what I think is the best of Blessingways — that they basically need nothing but intention. — Raven

My midwife explained the purpose of the Blessingway ceremony as being a ritual to honor the mother, to help prepare the mother for her hard work of labor and birth, and to pray for the safety of mother and baby. — Carla

I think the key is intention…for love and support. It's not just about buying something for the baby. — Diana

So much of this is an act of love and an act of creation, flexibility and responding to what's available. If we are holding positive intention, then we will come up with something that holds resonance. — Bronwen

A major impact

I felt incredibly special and supported and empowered. — Diana

The shock of labor kind of takes you by surprise, but when you've processed it and discussed it intimately, like in a Blessingway, then when you're in labor you remember that oh, yeah, other women have done this before me and I can do it too. — Merilynne

Religion plays a big part in my life. So it just didn't make sense to celebrate the miracle of life without God. For me, a typical baby shower has more emphasis on material goods than on spiritual gifts. I chose a Blessingway because I wanted to draw strength from praying together with my loved ones, and to get guidance from other Christian mothers as I entered this new arena of birth and parenting so that I could go into it with as much grace and wisdom and courage as possible. It was very spiritually uplifting, even more so than I imagined it would be.
  — Patricia

My friends planned a Blessingway ceremony for me during my third pregnancy. I had never heard of a Blessingway before, and I couldn't imagine it would be much different from a baby shower. But it was different. The Blessingway was not about getting ready for the material needs of the baby; instead it was all about honoring my womanhood, my motherhood, my value as a member of this community of women. It made me feel powerful enough to meet any challenge, but at the same time it made me realize that I would never have to face any challenge completely alone.
  — Margo

It was magnificent! I remember the woman, her name is Janet, she actually walked out of here "drunk," not having had any liquor. She said she couldn't even walk; she was so filled with so much love that she said it was a good thing we had planned to have her driven here and driven back to her own home.
— Nancy

It isn't everyday that one is treated so reverently as I was.
— Shelly

It feels so nurturing.
— Colette

I was covered in goosebumps during the entire ceremony and cried alot, the love and joy and gratitude washing over me and through me. I felt like I was getting ready for some huge and important work through the power of the ceremony, and I think my impending birth became real for me then.
— Francine

I'd like to be able to go back and do it again, sit in the room again…You can't capture something magical like that on video, but it would be nice to really physically sit there and savor it again and again.
— Carrie

It made me more relaxed and calm and made me feel more prepared. A Blessingway marks that transition from being pregnant to being a mother — with community support, with sisterhood, with empowerment, with people believing that you're capable of doing that. It helped me birth a baby rather than have a baby delivered, and I think there's a really big difference.
— Cindy

I felt believed in and loved and trusted at my Blessingway. It made me feel safer to go into the rest of the pregnancy and beyond. I knew that I would be okay and that the baby would be too.
— Lissa

My generation was born when our mothers were on Twilight Sleep and weren't aware of what took place, and there wasn't any kind of major connection. So doing the Blessingway is kind of a healing way for everybody to heal themselves and their own mothers and their children. Kind of heal past and present at the same time. And future. And setting the mood of "this is what birth could really be like" and that this kind of energy surrounding birth really does make a difference.   — Cindy

I never realized before that so many people loved me so much. And by the end of the ceremony, I actually felt like I deserved their love — which was an amazing new feeling for me! It really helped me have a positive attitude and therefore a more positive birth experience.
— Gabrielle

I remember at Jennifer's Blessingway, she cried and cried and cried, just to have that love and support. When you're pregnant, you're at such a vulnerable period of time in your life, and you're kind of scared and nervous. She did say afterward that she felt a little uncomfortable having all that attention focused on her, but at the same time she felt very special, very loved, with this great group of supportive people behind her in solidarity.   — Glenda

I felt really loved. I felt really accepted. I felt really empowered and supported and good.   — Laura

I really felt this connection with everybody that was there and it felt like a true celebration of the pregnancy and of me. It was a spiritual experience. I would have to say I really felt ready to have the baby — it was sort of like the last piece for me in my preparation to labor and give birth.   — Kathi

My first pregnancy I had so much time to just meditate, but with my second pregnancy, of course I had hardly a minute to do that. I think probably because of that, I actually had more fear about the second birth than the first. I just hadn't had time to process it, hadn't had time to confront it ahead of time. So the Blessingway for me was really a gift of time and of focus. I finally reached a point of relative equanimity thanks to those couple of hours of complete, reverent attention to this pregnancy, this labor, this baby.　　— Lynne

It helps to have that circle of support and know that those people are behind you spiritually before going into that space of aloneness that is being-in-labor, and having the pain or the power and physically giving birth. A Blessingway lets you give yourself that good energy before you go into that alone spot.　　— Mary

My first Blessingway was wonderful! I slept better that night than I did throughout the whole nine months. I felt so nurtured and loved — really special. I was honored for being a vessel, a home, for this new soul entering the earth plane.　　— Cindy Parker, in "The Blessingway"

The positive Blessingway energy stayed with me throughout the rest of my pregnancy. I carried that energy with me into labor. And now it's still with me every day, in my mothering.

　　— Karina

My Blessingway tuned me in to the fact that as a giver of life, I am connected to all mothers throughout history, including Mother Earth.

　　— Jamie

I felt so much more confident and surrounded and that there'd be somebody there to call afterwards. Those women show up again after the birth with meals and blueberry pies, so it's not just this isolated event. Everybody feels more connected.　　— Sandra

It all seems so meaningful.　　— Sarah

When women have a Blessingway, I think they carry over a lot of that strength of other women to the birth. As a midwife, I've seen the candles and other objects have a place of honor at the birth, and I think that makes a big difference in the mother's continuing to feel the support of everyone who was at her Blessingway. — Merilynne

We're whole people — body, mind, spirit, emotions and everything. The Blessingway engages all of that in the same way that birth does. So we get a practice run-through and a chance to go through whatever emotions it brings up. It's significant. It's a working-through. It's being able to accept being the center of attention. — Rahima

At first, I felt really embarrassed and awkward and shy. So did everyone else, I think, because in our culture we aren't usually so emotionally open and giving in our daily lives, and we certainly are never quite so touchy-feely! I guess I also felt undeserving of all this lavishing of love and attention. But by the end of the Blessingway ceremony, we all felt relaxed and comfortable, and I actually felt worthy of all the love and attention I got. I'm sure this helped me open up to my husband, my midwife and my doula during labor so that they could give me their support without my being inhibited about accepting it from them. I think it helped my friends and relatives open up too, so that they felt more free to be physically and emotionally demonstrative around me after the baby was born. Really, I think I got a whole ton more out of it than I might have otherwise gotten! — Heather

Afterward, when I would feel overwhelmed with anxiety, if I needed to I could close my eyes and meditate on the circle of women that was a reality, it wasn't a dream. And I could bring myself back to that, and it was very powerful and calming. I would envision you guys in a circle around me and I would feel safe. — Karina

There is so much data out there about doulas and the profound impact that the continuous presence of a caring mother-figure can have on a woman's labor. It just makes sense that a Blessingway brings the power of the "woman connection" to a birthing mother in much the same way. Especially if she has a candle, a yarn bracelet, or some other token from the Blessingway that she can bring with her to the birth, as a reminder that the love of all these people who care about her is right there with her.

— Roz

Women tell me [as their midwife] over and over again how wonderful the experience was of the Blessingway, of the ceremony, and how they felt more prepared and just felt like they could really open up. During the labor, during the birth, sometimes women will say, "I'm picturing the people that were there" or "I'm drawing on the energy from the Blessingway." People tell me afterward that it really helped them.

— Kathi

It was more of a ceremony than a shower. People didn't bring presents, but they brought things to read for me and we made this necklace. I really came out of it feeling strength from the women rather than coming out with bags of goodies. That was what was important to me at the time. It repowered me.

— Shelly

I wish I had had a Blessingway. It would have made such a big difference. If I had known in the last few weeks of my pregnancy that ten to fifteen women were out there wearing my bracelet and sending me good energy, I know I would have made it through so much easier. — Diana

It makes you feel special that so many people come together and say kind words. When you're pregnant, that's a period of time when you're feeling so unsure, their kind words about you help shore you up in preparation for the birth.

— Glenda

In life, your opportunities to discover that people really care about you are few and far between for the average person. When you have a Blessingway, it's like having a direct experience of their love. I think we lack that as a general rule, and the Blessingway is one of those rare moments when you get to actively experience it. I certainly did.

— Carol Ann

The pregnant woman should come out of her Blessingway with something that she can carry away, some physical manifestation of what went on there. What kind of impact do you think it would have if you were in the middle of a contraction and it was the three hundredth contraction and you were ready to give up and you looked down and you saw these women were symbolically with you. You know you can't stop the process, so where else do you turn to, where do you find your strength? You find it in the women who have vowed to be with you. It can remind you — we're all there, we're all with you. We can't take her pain away, we can't take the powerful transformation away, the only thing we can do is be there.

— Eleanor

It's amazing what the Blessingway does to people. Just amazing. It's very difficult to put into words. There's nothing like it that I know of for helping people prepare for birth. It just brings an incredible reality to it, and a power and an inner strength to the woman.

— Helen

The energy from my Blessingway was carried into the last days of my pregnancy.

— Melanie

It was very liberating — my fear was transformed into joy, and the power of love in the room made me feel open to the unpredictability of labor instead of vulnerable to it.

— Robin

Jill had a very hard time in labor but ultimately she had a triumphant birth. And as hard as her experience was, I think it would have been much much harder if she didn't have the Blessingway to draw on.

— Akiko

Building Community Connections

It declares to the community that you intend to raise this child together (which is an enormous undertaking — it's huge, it's really hard to do) and then in turn, it's asking that community for support. It's community building. That's how you keep a community together — you ask for support and you give support. I think Blessingways build emotional and community connections that way.
— Melisa

This Blessingway really highlighted where I was when I was pregnant this time. We knew we were really bringing this baby into a community. It was just incredible! I got to sit there that night in a room with these women from whom I had learned everything I knew about parenting, with the community who I share everything with, celebrate with, mourn with. It was very special to be able to look around the room and see that community that we had built for ourselves.
— Jennifer

We drive around in our cars which are little boxes that separate us; so many of us give birth in a hospital in a room with strangers; we die in rooms with strangers. It's a very isolating culture that we live in. I see really great value in bringing community together around a woman, and the Blessingway can serve that purpose. It can join her community of women friends around her, who can support her when she's about to go forth on her journey of giving birth.
— Mickey

I think it really cements community.
— Rahima

Becoming a mother used to be a community event, but now it's not. It's very isolating, especially for stay-at-home moms. The nurturing and ritual of a Blessingway can really bring a woman's community together to help her through this transition time. Women need that.
— Barbara

Different from baby showers

For me, it was perfect to have both a traditional baby shower and a Blessingway. At my baby shower, we received many of the gifts (baby paraphernalia) that we needed. It was a social event — I got to show off my beautiful big belly to all of my relatives. My Blessingway was a much more intimate experience. It was so fulfilling to have my closest friends there to help prepare me, emotionally and spiritually, for the upcoming birth.   — Kerry

I feel like baby showers have their place in our society, and they're very well-intentioned, but I do feel that what's missing from the baby shower is a welcoming of the baby on a spiritual level.   — Margo

At my shower, opening all those presents in front of everybody put a lot of pressure on me; it felt weird. But at my Blessingway, everybody else was in the spotlight as much as I was really. They were the ones that were reading and doing things; I was just taking it in. So that was a more comfortable way to receive.   — Stephanie

I see a Blessingway as being sacred and honoring the incredible spiritual process that's happening, as well as the physical process, and that isn't part of a baby shower generally. It's really honoring the mystery (and baby showers don't seem to be much about mystery!) I think we need more recognition of mystery. We need to really pause, to step outside of our regular lives and really let ourselves touch the mystery of being pregnant and growing this new life inside.   — Bronwen

A baby shower is about the baby. A Blessingway is more of an honoring of the woman and her journey. The gifts of a Blessingway really honor the mother. At a baby shower you don't receive oils for your feet and flowers for your hair, or poems to read. You receive functional items that you will use for your baby, which is important and it's lovely, but it doesn't feed the soul in the same way that a Blessingway does.   — Mickey

At my baby shower, I felt "on display" and very alone, even though I was surrounded by people who cared about me. The Blessingway was much more intimate and organic and deeply spiritual. There was so much love coming to me, and to the baby through me.   — Cathy

At a regular baby shower, you get presents and people are supportive, but a Blessingway is so much more. I think because it's not consumer-oriented, because it's more heart-oriented, it has a different feel to it.
            — Joanna

It seems like a baby shower is more about things, whereas a Blessingway is more about your spiritual self.   — Glenda

My Blessingway was a multicultural celebration. We added a new dimension to the baby shower process by borrowing from various traditions. Although my Blessingway ceremony was integrated into a conventional baby shower, I think a Blessingway could work either to replace or enhance a shower.   — Kira

From my perspective, a baby shower is usually a flurry of activity. But a Blessingway is a stillpoint — it feels as though time stops and the ceremony just is. There's no hurry, no hype, just a comfortable sense of being together and circulating love.   — Dionne

Ritual and Ceremony

Blessingway, ceremony, allows you to take time out of your life and take a different look at it. You're basically stopping your life and you're giving all of your attention to one thing.   — Raven

For me, ritual solidifies intent. Some things spiritually can't really be put into words, but the rituals in a Blessingway let us express them.

— Kate

Ritual is an exercise in going inward, into your soul, into your psyche, and then opening yourself up to let some of that out for good. So that's why you set your intention. I think it's a way to release or dig out energy and channel it for a good outcome. It allows us to reach out to generations past and present, because rituals can be steeped in tradition and passed on from generation to generation to generation. And when we do a ritual we are not only reaching back and touching our ancestors but we are also projecting this good energy into the future. What a wonderful way to welcome in a baby, by touching three generations or more, going back to the past and into the present and future.

— Dee

The meaning of ceremony is that it changes your life and it gives you whatever it is you're looking for — a witness of joy, or the strength to go on with a difficult situation, or an insight into something that was bewildering. It has that ability to give you those secret gifts that are not part of daily life.

— Raven

Giving birth is initiation into women's mysteries…it is a woman's vision quest, par excellence. The Vision Quest is a rite of passage for male members of some Native American Tribes. For young women, there is the Blessingway with a format more conducive for the task of mothering and natural childbirth. Natural childbirth itself can reveal the sustainable vision to spiritually support the mother for the rest of her life and Blessingway Ceremony prepares her for this vision.

— written by Jeannine Parvati Baker in *Prenatal Yoga and Natural Childbirth* and in private correspondence as a mother of six, midwife, and birthkeeper

Whenever you do ritual and create a sacred space, it's like you step out of time for a while. You're out of the hustle and bustle, you're stepping out of the daily grind and into that magical world where infinite possibilities exist. That's special.

— Cindy

The ceremony must be passed through publicly, i.e. ceremonially, so that the community can bear witness. This is an opportunity to make public that which one intends to leave behind and that which one intends to create for oneself. The community carries the memory, which helps to ground the transformation in reality.

— from *The Book of Ceremony* by Clem Gorman, with italicized words added by Raven Lang in *Blessingway into Birth*

Chants, Songs, and Sources of Music

These suggested chants, songs and sources of music for Blessingways come from a wide variety of religious and cultural traditions. I encourage you to adapt them to suit your needs; or, compose your own lyrics and/or music. Consider putting your words to the simple, pleasing tunes of folk songs or children's nursery rhymes.

Index of Chants and Songs — Alphabetical by Title

Angel of Love 192

As We Bless 206

(A) Blessing for Children (round) 213

Blessings on All Children 209

Child of Mine 204

(The) Circle Is Open 204

Dear Sister 190

Dream-Time 201

(The) Earth, the Air, the Fire, the Water 203

From a Woman 188

Funga 189

Goes Out Like a Wave 203

Help Her On Her Way 191

I Am a Hollow Bamboo 196

I Am Opening 194

I Am Walking in the Light of God 197

I Honor You (excerpt) 207

I Take Delight In 190

I Will Not Be Afraid 192

Let Me Open Like a Flower 194

Love Grows One By One 208

May the Blessings of the Goddess Rest Upon You 200

May Your Journey Be Blessed 214

(The) New Birthday Song 211

Our Sister 188

Power, Power, We Are Calling 191

Start the Day With Love 201

Strong As a Bear 195

There's Only One River 202

This Little Light of Mine 198

Time Is a River 200

We All Come From God 196

We All Come from the Goddess 197

We Are the Flow (excerpt) 193

We Are Sisters On a Journey 193

Welcome to This World 210

We've All Come to Welcome You 212

Where I Sit Is Holy 202

Woman, Wisdom 199

You Are Beautiful 189

Chants for Blessingways
Unless otherwise noted, these are folk songs passed down orally through the generations.

From a Woman

From a wo-man we were born in - to this cir - cle. From a

wo - man we were born in - to this world.

Our Sister

(Name) is our sis - ter, we must take care of her. (Name) is our

sis - ter, we must take care of her. Hey yon - na ho yon - na

hey yon yon, Hey yon-na ho yon-na hey yon yon.

In A *Blessingway*, Cynthia Burke suggests chanting this to a heartbeat rhythm, perhaps accompanied by drumming.

You Are Beautiful

(Name) you are beaut - i - ful, (Name) you are strong,

Won - der - ful to be with, carry us along (Name) here's our lov-ing song.

Funga

Traditional Nigerian. Music transcription and translation by Laz Slomovits of "Gemini." Reprinted with permission.

Fun - ga a - la - fi - a a - shay a - shay Fun - ga a - la - fi a a - shay a - shay

Fun - ga a la - fi - a a - shay a - shay Fun - ga a - la - fi - a a - shay a - shay. I

wel - come you in - to, in - to my heart. I wel - come you in - to, in - to my heart. I

wel - come you in to, in - to my heart. I wel - come you in to, in - to my heart.

I Take Delight In

Reprinted with permission from *Songs For Earthlings* ©1998 Julie Forest Middleton.
Published by Emerald Earth Publishing, Sebastopol California. www.EmeraldEarth.net

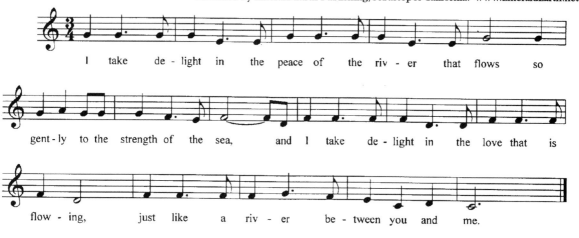

I take de-light in the peace of the riv-er that flows so gent-ly to the strength of the sea, and I take de-light in the love that is flow-ing, just like a riv-er be-tween you and me.

Dear Sister

Dear sis-ter, dear sis-ter, let me tell you how I'm-feel-ing.

You have giv-en us your treas-ure, we love you so.

Repeat, and/or sing in rounds. Or, try this variation introduced to me by midwife Nancy Wainer:

Dear baby, dear little baby, it is time for you to be born.

Your momma wants to nurse you, your daddy wants to hold you...

Help Her On Her Way

Sing additional verses with words such as *healing, breathing, pushing, family,* or *loving* in place of *birthing*.

Power, Power, We Are Calling

Music from *Circle of Song: Songs, Chants and Dances for Ritual and Celebration* (www.circleofsong.com). Reprinted by permission.

Other words, such as *courage*, can be substituted for *power*.

Angel of Love

An - gel   of love,   An - gel   of love, and she   comes when   we call,   An - gel   of love.

In "Sisters on a Journey," Sharon Glass suggests singing several verses, each with another word in place of love. She distributes Angel Cards which suggest words such as *faith* or *humor.*

I Will Not Be Afraid

Music from *Circle of Song: Songs, Chants and Dances for Ritual and Celebration* (www.circleofsong.com). Reprinted by permission.

I will not be a - fraid   to   feel all   my   fears   a - ny more.

I will not be a - fraid   to   feel all   my   fears   a - ny more.

I will not be a - fraid,   I will not be a - fraid.

from **We Are the Flow**

Shekhinah Mountainwater

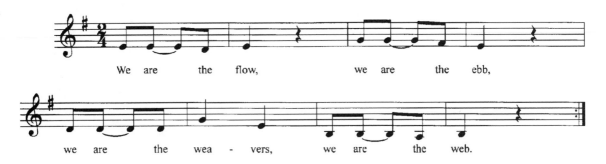

We are the flow, we are the ebb,

we are the wea - vers, we are the web.

Verse 2:
We are the weavers, we are the web, we are the spiders, we are the thread.

In *Circle of Song*, Kate Marks suggests linking hands and doing a weaving dance, perhaps using red yarn.

In *Women's Rituals*, Barbara Walker makes the following suggestion for symbolically weaving the web of sisterhood while chanting about it. Each person sitting or standing in the circle begins with a two-ounce ball of worsted wool knitting yarn that she then tosses to someone else in the circle. The receiver of each ball of yarn wraps the yarn once around her back, then tosses it to someone else. The web that forms in the center of the circle as the various strands of yarn crisscross will be so strong that it can hold the weight of the pregnant mother. She can lie across the middle as everyone else grasps the outer edges of the web and raises it up overhead, lifting her high off the ground. As Walker says, it's "always surprising to find how light even a heavy person can feel, when many are helping to lift. (If ten lift a 150-pound person, each is really lifting only 15 pounds!) It's also surprising to lie in the middle of such a web and find its apparent fragility transformed into dependable strength."

I Am Opening

I am o-pen-ing up in sweet sur-ren - der to the lu-min-ous love light

of the Lord. I am o-pen-ing up in sweet sur-ren - der to the lu-min-ous love light

of the Lord. I am o - pen - ing, I am o - pen - ing. I am

o - pen - ing, I am o - pen - ing.

Verse 2:
I am opening up in sweet surrender
to the luminous birthright of this babe.

Let Me Open Like a Flower

Lyrics by Paula Murphy. Music by **Kristi Bishop**.

Let me o-pen like a flower, flower, of love. life.

Strong As a Bear

Music by Nan Koehler

Oh Cre-a-tor, I am strong as a bear. Oh Cre-a-tor, I am strong as a bear.

Thank you, Cre-a-tor, I am strong. Oh Cre-a-tor, I am strong as a bear.

Ya - na yo-ni ya ho way ha nay Ya - na yo-ni ya ho way ha nay

yo-ni ya ho way ha nay hay ha nay Ya - na yo-ni ya ho way ha nay

I Am a Hollow Bamboo

Music by Nan Koehler

I am a holl-ow bam-boo. O-pen up, let light shine through.

Verse 2:
I am a hollow bamboo.
Open up, let the baby come through.

Verse 3:
I am a hollow bamboo.
Open up, love shines through.

We All Come From God

Music from *Songs of the Earth* by Anna Kealoha

We all come from God, and un - to God we shall re - turn.

Verse 2:
Like a ray of light, returning to the sun.

Verse 3:
Like a drop of water, flowing to the sea.

We All Come from the Goddess

Z. Budapest (www.zbudapest.com)

We all come from the God-dess, and to her we shall re - turn, like a

drop of rain, flow - ing to the o - cean.

I Am Walking in the Light of God

I am walk-ing in the light, in the light, in the light. I am walk-ing

in the light, in the light of God. In the light, in the light, in the light,

in the light, in the light, in the light, in the light of God.

This Little Light of Mine

Traditional African-American. Music transcription by Laz Slomovits of "Gemini." Reprinted with permission.

Verse 1:
Everywhere I go, I'm gonna let it shine (3x)
Let it shine, let it shine, let it shine.

Verse 2:
All over the world, I'm gonna let it shine (3X)
Let it shine, let it shine, let it shine.

Woman, Wisdom

Music from *Circle of Song: Songs, Chants and Dances for Ritual and Celebration* (www.circleofsong.com). Reprinted by permission.

Wo - man, wis - dom, wo - man   O   wey   O   wis - dom;
Ya   na   wa   na   ya   na   o   wey   o   ya   na

Wo - man, wis - dom, wo - man   O   wey   O   wis - dom;   Wo - man, wis - dom, wo - man   O
Ya   na   wa   na   ya   na   o   wey   o   ya   na   yo   na   wa   na   ya   na   o

wey   O   wis - dom;   Wo - man, wis - dom, wo - man   O   wey   O   wis - dom;
wey   o   ya   na   Ya   na   wa   na   ya   na   o   wey   o   ya   na

Wo - man, wis - dom, wo - man   O   wey   ho   hey   ne   yo   weh.
Ya   na   wa   na   ya   na   o   wey   ho   he   ne   yo   wey

Time Is a River

Julie Bos

Time is a riv-er and the riv-er flows free. Love is e-ter-nal like you and me. As

one we bring these spir-its to earth. Thank you for this chance to give birth.

May the Blessings of the Goddess Rest Upon You

Sufi Song

May the bless-ings of the Godd-ess rest up-on you. May Her peace a-bide in

you. May Her pre-sence ill-u-min-ate your heart now and for-ev-er more.

For a Judeo-Christian version, the word *Goddess* may be replaced with *God*.

Start the Day With Love

Satya Sai Baba

Start the day with love, spend the day with love,

end the day with love, sweet love, for that's the way to God.

Dream-Time

Oshia Drury

Dream - time, Dream - time. Wake up to the

Dream - time. Dream - time. Keep your feet on the ground and your

head in the stars. Dance your dream a - wake. Keep your

feet on the ground and your head in the stars. Dance your dream a - wake.

Dream your dance a - wake.

Where I Sit Is Holy

Music from *Songs to the Goddess* by Artemis College

Where I sit is ho - ly, ho - ly is this ground. For - est, moun - tain, riv - er,

lis - ten to the sound. Great spir - it cir - cles all a - round me.

In *Circle of Song*, Kate Marks suggests adding your own verses such as "Where we sing is holy, sacred is this place, as we breathe together, we fill with light and grace."

There's Only One River

There is on - ly one riv - er, there's on - ly one sea. And it's flow - ing through you and it's flow - ing through me. We are one. We are one.

The Earth, the Air, the Fire, the Water

The earth, the air, the fire, the wa-ter. Re-turn, re-turn, re-turn, re-turn. Ai

yay   ai yay   ai   yay   ai yay   ai   yo   ai yo   ai   yo   ai yo

Goes Out Like a Wave

Mickey Sperlich, midwife

Goes out like a   wave   and re-turns   to   the   cen - ter

repeat 4 times

Takes back what it   gave,   and re-news   it   at   the   cen - ter.

Child of Mine

Child of mine, bless-ed one, your jour-ney's been long and you're al-most home.

The Circle Is Open

Music from *Circle of Song: Songs, Chants and Dances for Ritual and Celebration* (www.circleofsong.com). Reprinted by permission.

The cir - cle is now o - pen, but un - bro - ken.

Mer - ry meet and mer - ry part, and mer - ry meet a - gain.

I particularly love this end-of-ceremony chant because it really expresses the essence of Blessingway — that the beneficent energy created on that day will be carried within each person, and will be felt every time they see or remember the honoree and one another.

Songs for Blessingways

We Are Sisters On a Journey

Marlena Fontenay. Reprinted by permission from *Circle of Song*.

We are sis - ters on a jour - ney, sing - ing now as one.

Shi - ning through the dark - est night, the heal - ing has be - gun, be - gun, the heal - ing has be - gun.

Verse 2:
We are sisters on a journey,
singing in the sun,
remembering the ancient ones,
the women and the wisdom,
the women and the wisdom.

Verse 3:
We are sisters on a journey
standing at the door,
remembering what passed long ago.
Let's turn the key once more.
Let's turn the key once more.

Verse 4:
We are sisters on a journey
watching life unfold,
sharing warmth of heart and hands,
the knowledge of the old,
the knowledge of the old.

In *Circle of Song*, Kate Marks suggests doing a circle dance to accompany this song. She says: "Dance in a circle, doing the grapevine step. (One step in front, one step in back.) As you step back, honor the past; as you step forward, honor the future. Hold hands throughout, raising and lowering them slowly in rhythm with the music. Think of the ebb and flow of life, of the bonding of women in sisterhood throughout time."

As We Bless

Faith Rogow. Reprinted with permission from *The Courage to Dare*.

As we bless the Source of Life, so we are blessed.

As we bless the Source of Life, so we are blessed. And the bless-ing gives us

strength, and makes our vis-ions clear. And the bless-ing gives us peace, and the

cour - age to dare. As we bless the Source of Life, so we are

blessed. As we bless the Source of Life, so we are blessed.

from **I Honor You**

Robert Gass. Reprinted with permission from *Trust in Love*.

Love Grows One By One

Carol Johnson, © 1981, Noeldner Music, BMI, 900 Calvin SE, Grand Rapids MI 49506. From the recording *Might As Well Make It Love*. Used by permission.

Blessings on All Children

Barbi Beyer

Bless-ings on all chil - dren and on our moth - er earth.

Bless - ings on cre - a - tion and the mir - a - cle of birth.

Bless - ing on (name) and on her child with - in.

Bless - ings on this fam - il - y and this new life to be - gin.

Welcome to This World

Robert Gass. Reprinted with permission from *Trust in Love*.

Refrain

Wel - come to this world, dear child. Wel - come to the

earth. All our love sur - rounds you at your birth. Though our

paths may some - day - part, right now you're too small to be a lone. So the

Verse

Lord has placed you in our home. When I see your ti - ny hands and

feet like pre - cious dew dops soft and sweet. And I see your eyes that

greet mine with out fear. How ev' ry mo - ment you're so ea - ger to

greet life a - new, I feel my heart just sings with love for you. (Refrain)

Verse 2:
I'd like to share with you a love for life
That God has shown to me.
I'd like to share with you
The hills, the sky, the sea.
To dance like waves upon the shoreline,
like stars on a summer's night,
Reflect the darkness with the glow of heaven's light.
(Refrain)

The New Birthday Song

Reprinted with permission from *Songs For Earthlings* ©1998 Julie Forest Middleton. Emerald Earth Publishing, Sebastopol CA (www.EmeraldEarth.net)

Hap - py birth - day, hap - py birth - day, just for you! Hap - py birth - day

and may all your dreams come true! When you blow out the can - dles,

one light stays a - glow, that's the love - light in your heart where - e'er you go!

Many women like to replace the words *just for you* with *we love you*. Julie Forest Middleton says, "I hate the birthday ritual where there's only one wish made and then the person blows germs all over the cake! Some years ago I made up another: everyone gets a votive candle and makes a wish (out loud) for the birthday person's next year. Then you all blow the candle flames out into the universe." This variation on the birthday cake ritual seems ideal for a Blessingway.

We've All Come to Welcome You

(All) We've all come to wel-come you, we'll all come to your birth. We've
all come to wel-come you, to wel-come you to Earth. (Mother) And I am here to
love you, I am here to love you. Yes, I am here to
love you, and give my bod-y for your quick and ea-sy
en - trance here through heav - en's o - pen door.

Fine

D.C. al Fine

A Blessing for Children (round)

Linda Hirschhorn, as recorded on *Roots and Wings* (Oyster Productions, Box 3929, Berkeley CA 94703). Reprinted with permission.

Sing verse 1 and 2, then go back to verse 1 to end the song.
The descant enters at the 5th measure ("keep") of verse 1 the last time (group 1 only).

May you be like the wa-tered gar-den, may you be like a flow-ing

stream, may you keep the mo-ment of wa-ken-ing from the heart of a per-fect dream.

Verse 2:
May the warmth of the Earth surround you,
may the passion of wonder fill your days,
may the strength of your friendship sustain you,
and your children be blessed always.

Descant

Voice

May they be a bless - ing, al - ways,

may they be a bless - - - - ing.

May Your Journey Be Blessed

Barbara Brookens Harvey

May your jour - ney be bless-ed; May you stay safe and warm. May the
Godd - ess pro - tect you on the day that you are born. Moth - er hold your
chil - dren tight, Moth - er lend your guid - ing light.

Suggested Sources of Music for Blessingways

  Birth Chants (compact disc)
Imani King
708-588-0275: www.WeavingtheWisdom.com

This powerful recording was made especially for Blessingways and births.

  Circle of Song: Songs, Chants and Dances for Ritual and Celebration
(songbook and/or compact disc or cassette)
Kate Marks, L.I.C.S.W. (Full Circle Press)
413-548-9884: www.crocker.com/~kmarks

This user-friendly songbook contains an extensive collection of ritual songs,
chants, dances, and meditations from all over the world.

⚶ *Mothersong — Little Blessings* (cassette)
Produced by Joya Winwood (Two Thumbs Up)
Can be ordered for $16, including shipping, directly from Joya Winwood at:
joyawinwood@got.net

Mothers, fathers, and children share the joy of song in this multicultural collection.

⚶ *Mother Divine* (compact disc)
Kurt Van Sickle (ISUN Music)
1-800-799-ISUN

This is a devotional choral chant in the goddess tradition, heralding Mother Divine for her gentleness, kindness, and eternal love.

⚶ *Returning* (compact disc)
Jennifer Berezan (Edge of Wonder Records)
www.edgeofwonder.com

The simple words *returning to the mother of us all* are repeated in a stirring chant that speaks to the womanspirit in each of us. Although this evocative recording does not lend itself easily to singing along, it is ideal for rituals such as the Moon Salutation.

⚶ *Ritual Songs* (cassette)
730 Pine Gold Hill, Boulder CO 80302-8756
(Proceeds support the Colorado Midwives Association)

American midwives' voices ring clear as they share some of their favorite ritual songs in a sing-along style.

 🜀 *Songs of the Earth* (songbook)
  Anna Kealoha (Celestial Arts)
  P. O. Box 15, Occidental CA 95472
  707-923-9642: www.bookwave.net

  Folk songs from a variety of religious and cultural traditions are shared in an easy-to-use format, which includes a beautiful selection of birthing songs and children's songs.

 🜀 *Songs for Earthlings: A Green Spirituality Songbook*
  Julie Forest Middleton (Emerald Earth)
  www.EmeraldEarth.net

  This is a comprehensive compilation of songs, rounds, and chants that honor and celebrate the many facets of life.

 🜀 *Songs to the Goddess, Strong as a Bear,* and *More Circle Songs* (cassettes)
  Recorded by Artemis College
  Available through Nan Koehler at:
  13140 Frati Ln., Sebastapol CA 95472

  These circle songs and chants are sung with clear voices and joyful hearts.

Sample Readings and Suggested Sources of Readings

Choosing readings is a very personal and intuitive process. I do not presume to tell you what will make the "best" readings for your Blessingway, but I would like to share a sampling of possibilities. What follows are some favorites of the women I interviewed.

Pregnancy and Birth

from Our Mother's Body is the Earth
Mary McAnally

Our mother's body is the earth,
her aura the air, her spirit
is in the middle, round like an egg,
and she contains all good things in herself,
like a honeycomb.

Birth is the pinnacle where women discover the courage to become mothers.
— Anita Diamant, from *The Red Tent*

The hips, they are wide for a reason, inside them is a satiny ivory cradle for new life. A woman's hips are outriggers for the body above and below; they are portals, they are a lush cushion, the handholds for love, a place for children to hide behind.
— Clarissa Pinkola Estes, from *Women Who Run With the Wolves*

You are preparing for the unknown, and once you are prepared, you are still before the doorway to the unknown. However, you are calm and relaxed at the entrance. You accept the unknown and accept the inability to control it, necessitating your yielding to it. Your strength lies in your confidence to open that door and begin the journey through unknown territory. This confidence influences the journey itself.

— This is a paraphrasing of a passage from *Birthing Normally* by Gayle Peterson

My friend Cindy shared the following affirmations aloud, then presented the mother with a stack of notecards inscribed with them.

Pregnancy affirmations:

- My body is beautiful and strong.
- My baby and I are ready for the divine plan of our lives to unfold.
- I love being pregnant.
- I have time for this pregnancy in my life.

Birth Affirmations:

- I send love to my baby and call him to my arms.
- I accept the healthy pain of labor, if and when it is here.
- I am opening.
- I am calm and relaxed. My baby feels my calmness and shares it.
- I am strong and I can let my contractions be strong.
- Strong contractions are good contractions.
- Contractions help my baby to be born.
- The baby and I are ready for the work we will do.
- My contractions are massaging the baby and hugging it.
- My body knows how to give birth and I will let it.
- I feel the love of those who are helping me.

Postpartum Affirmations:

- I share in the strength and wisdom of all mothers.
- I am adjusting to life with my new baby.
- I am a good parent to my child.
- My needs are important.

During normal childbirth your baby does not feel pain...The baby's sensation is one of healthy stimulation — stress but not distress. Your baby is massaged by your uterine contractions, and you may think of your contractions as hugging your baby, as he or she moves through labor...

Your baby's head molds easily, fitting through the cervix as it opens. You might imagine how pleasant it can feel to have hands cupped around your head, as often happens during a massage...And so it is for your baby...

Like many women, you may feel protective of your baby during labor. It can be comforting to visualize the normal labor process as a stimulating massage for your baby.   — Gayle Peterson, from *An Easier Childbirth*

No force of mind or body can drive a woman in labor; by patience only can the smooth force of nature be followed.
                                    — Grantly Dick-Read, from *Childbirth Without Fear*

Birth is not a beginning...The true beginning is at conception. Nor is birth an ending. It is more nearly a bridge between two stages of life, and although the bridge is not a long one, a child crosses it slowly, so that his body may be ready when he steps off at the far end.
                                    — Ashley Montagu, from *Life Before Birth*

Babies and Motherhood

Each child carries his own blessing into the world.
                                    — Yiddish Proverb

In the baby lies the future of the world. The mother must hold him close so he will know the world is his. The father must take him to the highest hill so he can see what his world is like.   — Mayan Indian saying

The Miracle
Maureen Hawkins

Before you were conceived
I wanted you
Before you were born
I loved you
Before you were here an hour
I would die for you
This is the miracle of life.

from **In the Waters of Intercourse — A Babylonian Birth Incantation**

The way is open for you,
the way is clear.
She will assist you,
She the creator,
She who created us all.

To the locks she will say,
"Be loosened,"
The doorsills are apart,
The door is raised.

As a desired child,
Bring yourself forth.

There are only two lasting bequests we can hope to give to our children. One of these is roots, the other, wings.　　　　　— Hodding Carter

Navajo Lullaby

The earth is your mother,
she holds you.
The sky is your father,
he protects you.
We are together always.
We are together always.
There never was a time when this was not so.

Waiting for You

MaryBeth Peters
(Written for her sister, who was preparing to adopt a little boy)

Though you were born in a faraway place,
Across the ocean there is already a space,
A home that is waiting to be filled by you.

Your first breath was taken, a gift from another,
The journey brings you home to the arms of your mother,
Arms that are waiting to be filled by you.

The journey seems long but it's almost done,
The life that is meant for you almost begun,
A life that is waiting to be filled by you.
A mother, a father, a sister wait here,
Hearts full of love for one already so dear,
Hearts that were waiting...now filled by you.

It takes a village to raise a child.   — African proverb

Inspirational

Imagine a Woman

Imagine a woman who

believes it is right and good she is a woman. A woman who honors her experience and tells her stories. Who refuses to carry the sins of others within her body and life.

Imagine a woman who

believes she is good. A woman who trusts and respects herself. Who listens to her needs and desires and meets them with tenderness and grace.

Imagine a woman who

has acknowledged the past's influence on the present. A woman who has walked through her past. Who has healed into the present.

Imagine a woman who

authors her own life. A woman who exerts, initiates, and moves on her own behalf. Who refuses to surrender except to her truest self and to her wisest voice.

Imagine a woman who

names her own gods. A woman who imagines the divine in her image and likeness. Who designs her own spirituality and allows it to inform her daily life.

Imagine a woman who

is in love with her own body. A woman who believes her body is enough, just as it is. Who celebrates her body and its rhythms and cycles as an exquisite resource.

Imagine a woman who

honors the face of God/Goddess in her changing face. A woman who celebrates the accumulation of her years and her wisdom. Who refuses to use precious energy disguising the changes in her body and her life.

Imagine a woman who

values the women in her life. A woman who sits in a circle of women. Who is reminded of the truth about herself when she forgets.

Imagine Yourself as This Woman

Serenity Prayer

God grant me the serenity to accept the things I cannot change, the courage to change the things I can, and the wisdom to know the difference.

Blessed Be...
Extract from "The Network of the Imaginary Mother"
from *Lady of the Beasts: Poems by Robin Morgan*
Copyright © 1976 by Robin Morgan
By permission of Edite Kroll Literary Agency, Inc.

Blessed be my brain
    that I may conceive of my own power.
Blessed be my breast
    that I may give sustenance to those I love.
Blessed be my womb
    that I may create what I choose to create.
Blessed be my knees
    that I may bend so as not to break.
Blessed be my feet
    that I may walk in the path of my highest will.

Love conquers all things; let us too surrender to love. — Virgil

Suggested Sources of Readings for Blessingways

I have found the following to be fruitful sources of readings. You will find many more gems if you explore the internet or browse in your local bookstores. Or write your own letter, story, song, or poem for the occasion.

- ⚚ *The Tao of Motherhood* by Vimala McClure (Willow Springs, MO: NUCLEUS Publications, 1994) — Offers philosophical insights into the mysteries of motherhood.

- ⚚ *Celebrating Motherhood: A Comforting Companion for Every Expecting Mother* by Andrea Alban Gosline and Lisa Burnett Bossi with Ame Mahler Beanland (Berkeley, CA: Conari, 2002) — A diverse compilation of homages to pregnancy, birth, mothers, and children.

- ⚚ *Mothering* — This parenting magazine includes poetry as well as thought-provoking ruminations from the editor.

- ⚚ *The Compleat Mother* — Poetry and inspirational stories are included in this vocally pro-attachment-parenting magazine.

- ⚚ *MotherPrayer: The Pregnant Woman's Spiritual Companion* by Tikva Frymer-Kensky (NY: Riverhead Books, 1996) — A thoughtful examination of how people from many religious traditions express the emotions of pregnancy, birth and motherhood.

- ⚚ Children's storybooks such as *On the Day You Were Born* by Debra Frasier (San Diego: Harcourt Brace Jovanovich, 1991).

VI

THE FABRIC SHOP

Recommended Reading: More Information About Blessingways

To find out more about the Blessingway concept, look for these resources. Ask your local librarian to help you access these titles through Interlibrary Loan.

⚬ *Seasons of Change: Growing Through Pregnancy and Birth*
Suzanne Arms (Kivaki Press)

In this lovely photo-diary of everywoman's pregnancy, the pregnant woman is gifted with a Blessingway.

⚬ "Rituals for Birth: The Blessingway Ceremony,"
Jeannine Parvati Baker
from: *The Goddess Celebrates: An Anthology of Women's Rituals*
edited by Diane Stein (Freedom, CA: Crossing Press, 1991)
See www.freestone.org or www.birthkeeper.com to read this and other writings by Jeannine Parvati Baker online.

This description of a Blessingway ceremony closely adheres to the Navajo traditional ways as they were interpreted by the modern American midwifery community.

⚭ *A Blessingway: A Very Special Baby Shower*
Cynthia Burke (Wakefield, RI: Greenwood Press, 1996)
Order directly from the author at:
70 Chestnut Hill Rd., Wakefield RI 02879

A surprise Blessingway ceremony is outlined in replicable detail in this little booklet, which includes fresh ideas such as a serenade of the pregnant mother.

⚭ *Ceremonies for Real Life: Ten Ways to Bring the Sacred to All Occasions*
Carine Fabius (Tulsa, OK: Council Oak, 2003)

The author designed and scripted heartfelt ceremonies for each of life's major transitions. She also offers a "New Baby Ceremony Kit" through Lakaye Mehndi Studio: (323)460-7333.

⚭ "Sisters on a Journey"
Sharon Glass (*Midwifery Today*, January 1991, No. 17)

One woman's Blessingway is described in vivid detail.

⚭ *Welcoming Ways: Creating Your Baby's Welcome Ceremony with the Wisdom of World Traditions*
Andrea Alban Gosline (San Rafael, CA: Cedco, 1999)

This is a treasure trove of ideas for baby-oriented Blessingways.

⚭ *The Heart of the Circle: A Guide to Drumming*
Holly Blue Hawkins (Freedom, CA: Crossing Press, 1999)

This brilliant little gem is not just a book about drumming! It explores the role of ceremony, community and music in modern American life. The why's and how's of creating a ceremony such as a Blessingway are also examined with depth, clarity, and insight.

⚭ "Celebration of the Mother: Blessingways for Women Giving Birth"
Lucinda Herring (Chinaberry Books)
To order this article, please call: (800) 776-2242

A lot of ideas are packed into just a few pages, as Waldorf educator Lucinda Herring shares her own discoveries about Blessingways.

⚭ *Womanspirit: A Guide to Women's Wisdom*
Hallie Iglehart Austen (San Francisco: Harper & Row, 1983)

This is a thoughtful guide to creating new rituals based upon our spiritual heritage as women.

⚭ "Blessingway"
Raven Lang
from: *Artemis Speaks: VBAC Stories and Natural Childbirth Information*
edited by Nan Koehler (Sebastapol, CA: Nan Koehler, 1989)

Legendary midwife Raven Lang, who, inspired by her friend Betsy Herbert, first introduced the Blessingway concept to mainstream America, offers valuable insights into the magic and power of Blessingway ceremonies.

⚭ *Blessingway Into Birth, A Rite of Passage*
Raven Lang (Santa Cruz, CA: Raven Lang, 1993)
To order this booklet, please send $15 to:
Raven Lang, 225 Forest Ave. Santa Cruz, CA 95062

This groundbreaking booklet contains the first teachings about Blessingways written by a non-Navajo. It includes a collection of stories about women's Blessingway experiences, an analysis of the hidden mysteries and prophetic qualities of each ceremony, and an evaluation of the benefits of Blessingways.

⚭ *A Ceremonies Sampler: New Rites, Celebrations, and Observances of Jewish Women*
Elizabeth Reznick Levine (San Diego: Women's Institute for Continuing Jewish Education, 1991)

Modern Jewish women share their own stories about weaving religious traditions and feminine spiritual needs together to create new ceremonies for a variety of rites of passage.

⚭ *Water Birth: A Midwife's Perspective*
Susanna Napierala (Westport, CT: Bergin & Garvey, 1994)

From using water in labor to guiding pregnant women through the transition of birth with woman-to-woman ceremonies, the author encourages a return to a more natural, instinctive approach to childbirth.

⚭ *Casting the Circle: A Women's Book of Ritual*
Diane Stein (Freedom, CA: Crossing Press, 1990)

This is a thoughtful examination of the philosophy, herstory, and politics behind women today reclaiming "the goddess within" through ritual.

⚭ "The Blessingway: An Alternative Baby Shower"
Sue Robins (*Canadian Women's Health Network*, Winter 2001, Volume 4, Number 1. Available online at www.cwhn.ca)

The author reminisces about the first Blessingways she shared with her friends, who were accustomed to conventional baby showers.

  ◡ "Beads and Blessings"
     Anne Nicholson Weber
     (*Mothering* online: www.mothering.com/11-0-0/html/11-2-0/blessingway.shtml)

     This author tells her own powerful Blessingway story.

  ◡ *Blessing the Way* (video with companion guidebook)
     Laura Scheerer Whitney (Ojai, CA: Sage Mountain Films, 1998)
     To order please call (805)640-6961 or visit their website at
     www.sagemtnfilms.com

     The essence of two deeply healing Blessingways is captured on videotape.

Other Selected Resources for a Holistic Approach to Pregnancy, Childbirth and Parenting

Organizations and Websites

⚠ ABC's of Parenting webpage
www.abcparenting.com

An extensive listing of websites pertinent to new parents

⚠ ALACE (Association of Labor Assistants and Childbirth Educators)
www.alace.org; (617)441-2500

Referrals to local doulas and childbirth educators

⚠ Alliance for Transforming the Lives of Children
www.atlc.org; (888) 574-7580

An international coalition of individuals and organizations committed to promoting the physical and emotional well-being of children

⚠ Association for Pre- & Perinatal Psychology and Health
www.birthpsychology.com; P.O. Box 1398, Forestville CA 95436

Information and ideas about the "mental and emotional dimensions" of pregnancy, birth, and parenting

⚠ At-Home Mothers
www.AtHomeMothers.com; 406 E. Buchanan Ave., Fairfield IA 52556

Practical, emotional, and financial support for at-home mothers

⚘ Birth and Life Bookstore
www.1cascade.com/bookstore; (800)443-9942; 141 Commercial Street NE, Salem OR 97301

A mail-order catalog of over 5,000 current and classic titles relating to pregnancy, birth, and parenting

⚘ Birthing the Future
www.birthingthefuture.com; (970)884-4090

Renowned activist, author and filmmaker Suzanne Arms dispels common myths about childbirth and breastfeeding, supported by research citations and recommended resources

⚘ BirthWorks
www.birthworks.com; (888)TO-BIRTH

Certifies and makes referrals to childbirth educators and doulas

⚘ Childbirth and Postpartum Professionals Association (CAPPA)
www.childbirthprofessional.com; (888)548-3672

Certifies and makes referrals to childbirth professionals such as childbirth educators; labor and postpartum doulas; lactation consultants and others

⚘ Childbirth website
www.childbirth.org

Information about pregnancy and childbirth, including an outstanding guide to birth plans

⚚ Coalition for Improving Maternity Services
www.motherfriendly.org; (888)282-CIMS

This well-respected collaborative effort between doctors, midwives, and other maternity service providers offers free informational materials such as "The Mother-Friendly Childbirth Initiative" and "Having a Baby? Ten Questions to Ask"

⚚ The Cochrane Collaboration
www.cochrane.org

Reviews of current medical literature

⚚ Cutting Edge Press
www.birthballs.com

A select collection of books, music, videos, and other products for childbirth professionals and pregnant women

⚚ Dr. Sears
www.askdrsears.com

Baby care recommendations and parenting advice from renowned pediatrician Dr. William Sears

⚚ Doulas of North America (DONA)
www.dona.org; (888)788-DONA

Information about doulas and other birth-related issues, and referrals to local doulas

International Cesarean Awareness Network (ICAN)
⚚ www.ican-online.org; (310) 542-6400
"Works to lower the rate of unnecessary cesareans, supports VBAC, and

encourages positive birthing through education and advocacy"; offers online and local support groups for women who have given birth by cesarean section

⚳ International Childbirth Education Association (ICEA)
www.icea.org; (952)854-8660

Referrals to childbirth educators, postnatal educators, doulas, and perinatal fitness educators; extensive catalog of books, videos, and other educational materials about pregnancy, birth, and parenting

⚳ International Lactation Consultants Association
www.ilca.org; (919)861-5577

Referrals to lactation consultants

⚳ Lamaze International
www.lamaze.org; (800)368-4404

Referrals to a variety of childbirth and early parenting resources; extensive catalog of educational materials about pregnancy, birth, and parenting

⚳ La Leche League (LLL)
www.laleche.org; (800)LA-LECHE

Information about breastfeeding, and referrals to local woman-to-woman support groups

⚳ Maternity Center Association
www.maternity.org; (212)777-5000

Their "Maternity Wise: Helping Women Make Informed Decisions" program offers printed informational materials as well as an extensive and well-balanced webpage

⚕ Midwifery Today
www.midwiferytoday.com; (800)743-0974

A magazine for midwives that reaches out to parents too, especially on its website

⚕ Midwifery webpage
www.midwifeinfo.com

Information about midwifery

⚕ Midwives Alliance of North America (MANA)
www.mana.org; (888)MID-WIFE

Referrals to local midwives

⚕ Mothers and More
www.mothersandmore.org; (630)941-3553

Support and advocacy for mothers, with an emphasis on helping women balance career and family

⚕ Motherwear
www.motherwear.com; (800)950-2500

A clothing catalog, but also a source of free booklets on breastfeeding topics such as nursing in public, the first six weeks, going back to work, and the family bed

⚕ National Association of Childbearing Centers (NACC)
www.birthcenters.org, or send $1 to:
NACC, 3123 Gottschall Rd., Perkionville PA 18074

Referrals to local birthing centers

⚘ National Association of Postpartum Care Service
www.napcs.org; (800)45-DOULA

Referrals to nonmedical postpartum caregivers

⚘ National Organization of Circumcision Information Resource Centers (NoCIRC)
www.nocirc.org; (415)488-9883

Information about circumcision and the movement to end it

⚘ National Vaccine Information Center: Americans for Vaccine Safety and
Accountability (NVIC)
www.909shot.com; (800)909-SHOT

Advocates parental freedom to make informed, individualized vaccination
decisions for their children

⚘ The Natural Child Project
www.naturalchild.org; (866) 593-1547

Information, resources, and encouragement for respectful parenting

⚘ Parenting Concepts
www.parentingconcepts.com; (909)609-9005

Offers slings and other attachment parenting products along with free
information about babywearing and cosleeping

⚘ Parents Place webpage
www.parentsplace.com

Articles about topics pertinent to new parents

- Postpartum Support International
www.postpartum.net; (805)967-7636 or (818)887-1312

  A volunteer support network for women with postpartum depression

- Primal Health Research Centre
www.birthworks.org/primalhealth; c/o Dr. Michel Odent, 72 Savernake Rd. London, England NW3 2JR

  Promotes and disseminates research about correlations between the primal period (fetal, perinatal, and early infancy experiences) and human health later in life

Books, Magazines, and Videos

Pregnancy and Birth

- *Active Birth: The New Approach to Giving Birth Naturally*
Janet Balaskas (Harvard, MA: Harvard Common Press, 1992)

  Definitely my favorite birth book

- *Birth as an American Rite of Passage*
Robbie Davis-Floyd (Berkeley, CA: University of California Press, 2004)

  An anthropological study of the modern U.S. hospital birth experience

- *The Birth Book: Everything You Need to Know to Have a Safe and Satisfying Birth*
Dr. William Sears (Boston: Little, Brown & Co., 1994)

  A straightforward parents' handbook

⚸ *The Birth Partner: Everything You Need to Know to Help a Woman Through Childbirth*
Penny Simkin (Boston: Harvard Common Press, 2001)

Popular with dads

⚸ *Birth Reborn* (book)
Michel Odent (Medford, NJ: Birth Works Press, 1994)

A documented critique of routine medical interventions during labor, and an outline of natural alternatives for obstetricians and midwives

⚸ *Birth Reborn* (video)
Michel Odent (Films, Inc.)

A French obstetrician attends several hospital births, including a cesarean birth, and explores what factors make these births such positive experiences

⚸ *Birthing From Within: An Extra-Ordinary Guide to Childbirth Preparation*
Pam England and Rob Horowitz (Albuquerque: Partera Press, 1998)

A guided journey of self-discovery that encourages approaching pregnancy, birth and parenting with awareness and insight

⚸ *The Complete Book of Pregnancy and Childbirth* (also any other title by this prolific author)
Sheila Kitzinger (NY: Alfred A. Knopf, 2004)

A lovely (and practical) guide to the childbearing year

⚸ *The Doula Book: How a Trained Labor Companion Can Help You Have a Shorter, Easier, and Healthier Birth*

Marshall Klaus, John Kennell, and Phyllis Klaus (Cambridge, MA: Perseus Publishing, 2002)

A clear and convincing documentation of the benefits of labor support

⚕ *An Easier Childbirth: A Mother's Workbook for Health and Emotional Well-Being During Pregnancy and Delivery*
Gayle Peterson (Berkeley, CA: Shadow & Light, 1994)

Journal questions, guided visualizations and other useful exercises that can help women prepare physically and psychologically for birth

⚕ *Essential Exercises for the Childbearing Year: A Guide to Health and Comfort Before and After Your Baby is Born*
Elizabeth Noble (Harwich, MA: New Life Images, 2003)

Lots of helpful information about taking care of yourself and your baby, including illustrations and an extensive resource directory

⚕ *Get Through Childbirth in One Piece: How to Prevent Episiotomies and Tearing*
Elizabeth Bruce (San Jose, CA: Writer's Club Press, 2001)

A convincing and encouraging summary of how and why women can take responsibility for their own births

⚕ *Gentle Birth Choices: A Guide to Making Informed Decisions About Birthing Centers, Birth Attendants, Water Birth, Home Birth, Hospital Birth* (book)
Barbara Harper (Rochester, VT: Healing Arts Press, 1994)

Challenges our routine medical approach to childbirth and encourages compassionate and safe alternatives such as waterbirth

    Gentle Birth Choices (video)
Barbara Harper (Vision Quest Video, 2000)

The triumphant births are not to be missed, whether or not you agree with the politics of this video

    A Good Birth, a Safe Birth: Choosing and Having the Childbirth Experience You Want
Diane Korte and Roberta Scaer (Harvard, MA: Harvard Common Press, 1992)

A practical guide to navigating the sea of childbirth options

    Having a Baby, Naturally: The Mothering Magazine Guide to Pregnancy and Childbirth
Peggy O'Mara (NY: Atria Books, 2003)

An up-to-date overview of birthing options, with an extensive resource guide

    Hygieia: A Woman's Herbal
Jeannine Parvati (Baker) (Berkeley, CA: Freestone Publications, 1978)

A compendium of plant lore using herbs for Blessingways and other women's healing ceremonies

    Immaculate Deception II: Myth, Magic & Birth
Suzanne Arms (Berkeley, CA: Celestial Arts, 1996)

A brilliant exposé of the failures of modern American obstetrics

    Mind Over Labor: How to Reduce the Fear and Pain of Childbirth Through Mental Imagery
Carl Jones (NY: Penguin, 1988)

A guide to using visualization techniques in pregnancy and birth

⚘ *The Natural Pregnancy Book: Herbs, Nutrition and Other Holistic Choices*
Aviva Jill Romm (Berkeley, CA: Celestial Arts, 2003)

A codification of traditional midwives' wisdom, from herbal remedies to Blessingways

⚘ *The Nurturing Touch at Birth: A Labor Support Handbook*
Paulina Perez (Katy, TX: Cutting Edge Press, 1997)

For fathers, friends, and doulas who want practical advice about "being there" for a woman in labor

⚘ *Pregnant Feelings: Developing Trust in Birth*
Rahima Baldwin and Terra Palmarini Richardson (Berkeley, CA: Celestial Arts, 1990)

A workbook that facilitates emotional well-being during the childbearing year

⚘ *The Pregnant Woman's Comfort Book: A Self-Nurturing Guide to Your Emotional Well-Being During Pregnancy and Early Motherhood*
Jennifer Louden (San Francisco: Harper Collins, 1995)

This gentle examination of the emotional and spiritual impact of bringing a baby into the world offers practical advice for self-nurturing during pregnancy

⚘ *The Pregnant Woman's Companion: Nine Strategies That Work to Keep Your Peace of Mind Through Pregnancy and Into Motherhood*
Christine D'Amico and Margaret Taylor (Minneapolis, MN: Attitude Press, 2002)

An overview of the emotional challenges pregnancy can bring and the most effective strategies for coping with them

   ⚜ *Prenatal Yoga and Natural Childbirth*
Jeannine Parvati Baker (Monroe, UT: Freestone Publications, 2001)

The first book to integrate yoga and birth, acknowledging both as powerful spiritual initiations. Written in 1974, then expanded and revised in 2001 with the author's Blessingway ceremonies for her six children

   ⚜ *Spiritual Midwifery*
Ina May Gaskin (Summertown, TN: Book Publishing Co., 2002)

A timeless collection of triumphant homebirth stories

   ⚜ *The Thinking Woman's Guide to a Better Birth*
Henci Goer (NY: Berkeley Publishing Group, 1999)

An in-depth analysis of standard medical interventions

   ⚜ *Understanding Diagnostic Tests of the Childbearing Year: A Holistic Guide to Evaluating the Health of Mother and Baby*
Anne Frye (Portland, OR: Labrys Press, 1997)

A detailed evaluation of the major tests

   ⚜ *Wise Woman Herbal for the Childbearing Year*
Susan Weed (Woodstock, NY: Ash Tree, 1986)

A layperson's guide to herbs for pregnancy, birth, and postpartum care

   ⚜ *Yoga for Pregnancy: Safe and Gentle Stretches*
Sandra Jordan (NY: St. Martin's Press, 1987)

Simple, well-illustrated tips for safely and comfortably stretching, strengthening, and relaxing the pregnant body

Babies and Parenting

 ⚹ *After the Baby's Birth...A Woman's Way to Wellness: A Complete Guide for Postpartum Women*
Robin Lim (Berkeley, CA: Celestial Arts, 2001)

Valuable advice about nurturing mothers and babies during the "fourth trimester"

 ⚹ *Your Amazing Newborn*
Marshall Klaus and Phyllis Klaus (Cambridge, MA: Perseus Publishing, 2002)

An intriguing photo-essay that "shows parents everything a newborn can see, hear, taste, smell and feel in the first minutes and weeks of life"

 ⚹ *The Baby Book: Everything You Need to Know About your Baby From Birth to Age Two*
Dr. William Sears (Boston: Little, Brown, 2003)

My favorite comprehensive parenting guide (other superlative titles by this prolific author include *Nighttime Parenting* and *The Discipline Book*)

 ⚹ *Bonding: Building the Foundations of Secure Attachment and Independence*
Marshall Klaus, John Kennell, and Phyllis Klaus (Cambridge, MA: Perseus Publishing, 1995)

A well-researched examination of the factors that influence parent-infant bonding

 ⚹ *Breastfeeding Your Baby*
Sheila Kitzinger (NY: Alfred Knopf, 1998)

A user-friendly guidebook packed with great photographs

⚘ *Circle Round: Raising Children in Goddess Traditions*
Starhawk, Diane Baker, and Anne Hill (NY: Bantam, 2000)

A treasure trove of information and ideas; especially designed to guide and support parents who practice earth-honoring religions, but most of the child-friendly crafts and rituals will appeal to a wider audience as well

⚘ *The Circumcision Decision* (pamphlet)
Edward Wallerstein
Order through ICEA (see Organizations, above)

A straightforward risk/benefit analysis of newborn circumcision

⚘ *The Compleat Mother* (Magazine)
(701)852-2822, www.CompleatMother.com

An outspoken Canadian mouthpiece for homebirth, attachment parenting, breastfeeding, and other "alternative" choices

⚘ *Conscious Conception: Elemental Journey Through the Labyrinth of Sexuality*
Jeannine Parvati Baker (Monroe, UT: Freestone Publications, 1986)

A comprehensive guidebook toward making every baby a welcomed baby through fertility awareness, natural parenting, and ceremony

⚘ *The Continuum Concept: In Search of Lost Happiness*
Jean Liedloff (Reading, MA: Addison-Wesley, 1995)

A fascinating anthropological study of the way the Stone Age Indians of South America raise their children

⚘ *The Family Bed: An Age Old Concept in Child Rearing*
Tine Thevenin (NY: Perigee, 2003)

The original co-sleeping handbook

⚭ *The Five Love Languages: How to Express Heartfelt Commitment to Your Mate*
Gary Chapman (Chicago: Northfield, 1995)

The focus is on healing marital conflict, but I have found that the strategies offered are equally helpful for optimizing parent-child relationships

⚭ *The Hip Mama Survival Guide*
Ariel Gore (NY: Hyperion, 1998)

Razor-sharp "advice from the trenches" on pregnancy, childbirth, and a tangle of parenting joys and challenges including breastfeeding, divorce, poverty, and being a feminist mother

⚭ *Hip Mama: The Parenting Zine*
www.hipmama.com

More of the above, in an online magazine

⚭ *Home Education Magazine*
(800)236-3278; www.home-ed-magazine.com

The premiere magazine of its kind, packed with information and inspiration for the great diversity of homeschoolers

⚭ *How Children Learn* (or any other title by this brilliant author)
John Holt (Reading, MA: Addison-Wesley, 1997)

An especially insightful look at the magical process of child development and the influence adults have upon it

⚘ *How to Raise a Healthy Child in Spite of Your Doctor*
Dr. Robert Mendelsohn (NY: Ballantine, 1987)

A no-nonsense guide to making the best health care decisions for each individual child

⚘ *How to Talk So Kids Will Listen & Listen so Kids Will Talk*
Adele Faber and Elaine Mazlish (NY: Quill, 2002)

Readable, usable advice about how to communicate effectively with children

⚘ *Infant Massage: A Handbook for Loving Parents*
Vimala Schneider McClure (NY: Bantam, 2000)

A sweet introduction to the why's and how's of infant massage

⚘ *Mothering*
(800)984-8116, www.mothering.com

An outstanding "alternative" parenting magazine that lovingly embraces a diverse readership

⚘ *The Nursing Mother's Companion*
Kathleen Huggins (Boston: Harvard Common Press, 1999)

A clearly written and illustrated guide to breastfeeding

⚘ *Raising Your Spirited Child: A Guide for Parents Whose Child Is More Intense, Sensitive, Perceptive, Persistent, Energetic*
Mary Sheedy Kurcinka (NY: HarperPerennial, 1998)

Positive strategies for parenting children with challenging temperamental traits

⚜ *Siblings Without Rivalry: How to Help Your Children Live Together So You Can Too*
Adele Faber and Elaine Mazlish (NY: Quill, 2002)

Insightful guidelines for fostering positive sibling interactions

⚜ *So That's What They're For: Breastfeeding Basics*
Janet Tamaro (Holbrook, MA: Adams Media, 1998)

Both funny and factual

⚜ *Tears and Tantrums: What to Do When Babies and Children Cry*
Aletha Solter (Goleta, CA: Shining Star Press, 1998)

A developmental psychologist explains why children cry and how parents can deal with it

⚜ *Trust the Children: A Manual and Activity Guide for Homeschooling and Alternative Learning*
Anna Kealoha (Berkeley, CA: Celestial Arts, 1995)

A comprehensive guide to learning both academics and non-academics together as a family

⚜ *Vaccinations: A Thoughtful Parent's Guide*
How to Make Safe, Sensible Decisions About the Risks, Benefits, and Alternatives
Aviva Jill Romm (Rochester, VT: Healing Arts Press, 2001)

An intelligent examination of the complicated subject of childhood vaccines

 ⚭ *Watch Me Grow: I'm One-Two-Three: A Parent's Essential Guide to the Extraordinary Toddler to Preschool Years*
Maureen O'Brien and Sherill Tippins (NY: Quill, 2002)

Helps parents understand and appreciate each developmental stage

 ⚭ *The Womanly Art of Breastfeeding*
(Schaumburg, IL: La Leche League International, 2004)

The classic breastfeeding guide

 ⚭ *Welcoming the Soul of a Child*
Jill E. Hopkins (New York: Kensington Books, 1999)

An offering of heartfelt rituals to inspirit the conception, birth, and life of a child

BIBLIOGRAPHY

Alban Gosline, Andrea. *Welcoming Ways: Creating Your Baby's Welcome Ceremony with the Wisdom of World Traditions*. San Rafael, CA: Cedco, 1999.

Banack, Connie. "Blessing Way Ceremonies: A Celebration." www.mother-care.ca.

Blue Hawkins, Holly. *The Heart of the Circle: A Guide to Drumming*. Freedom, CA: Crossing Press, 1999.

Burke, Cynthia. *A Blessingway: a very special baby shower*. Wakefield, RI: Greenwood Press, 1996.

Cooke, Courtney. *The Best Baby Shower Book: A Complete Guide for Party Planners*. New York: Meadowbrook, 1986.

Cornell, Laura. "The Moon Salutation: Expression of the Feminine in Body, Psyche, Spirit," masters thesis, Oakland, CA, 2000 (Available through UMI Dissertations Publishing, Ann Arbor, Michigan).

Davis, Elizabeth and Carol Leonard. *The Circle of Life: Thirteen Archetypes for Every Woman*. Berkeley, CA: Celestial Arts, 1996.

Diamant, Anita. *The Red Tent*. New York: St. Martin's Press, 1997.

Dick-Read, Grantly. *Childbirth Without Fear: The Original Approach to Natural Childbirth*. New York: Harper & Row, 1959.

England, Pam and Rob Horowitz. *Birthing From Within: An Extra-Ordinary Guide to Childbirth Preparation*. Albuquerque: Partera Press, 1998.

Fabius, Carine. *Celebrating with Ceremony* (kit and handbook). LA, CA: Lakaye Mehndi Studio, 2000.

Farrell, Edward J. *Celtic Meditations*. Denville, NJ: Dimension Books, 1976.

Glass, Sharon. "Sisters on a Journey." *Midwifery Today* 17 (January 1991): 18 - 19.

Gorman, Clem. *The Book of Ceremony*. Bottisham, Cambridge: Whole Earth Tools, 1972.

Grenier Sweet, Gail. "Blessingway." *Mothering* (Winter 1982).

Hawkins, Maureen. "The Miracle" in *Ain't I a Woman! A Book of Women's Poetry from*

Around the World, ed. Illona Linthwaite. New York: Peter Bedrick Books, 1988.

Heerens Lysne, Robin. *Dancing Up the Moon: A Woman's Guide to Creating Traditions That Bring Sacredness to Daily Life*. Berkeley, CA: Conari, 1995.

Hopkins, Jill E. *Welcoming the Soul of a Child*. New York: Kensington Books, 1999.

Jackson, Deborah. *With Child: Wisdom and Traditions for Pregnancy, Birth, and Motherhood*. San Francisco: Chronicle Books, 1999.

Kent Rush, Anne. *Moon, Moon*. Berkeley, CA: Moon Books, 1976.

Koehler, Nan, Marilyn Murphy, and Madrone Williams. "Blessingway (California Style)." Working paper, compiled 1982 - 1992. Available from Nan Koehler at (707)874-2315 or nan@rainbowsendfarm.com.

Lang, Raven. "Blessingway" in *Artemis Speaks: VBAC Stories and Natural Childbirth Information*, ed. Nan Koehler, 536 - 541. Sebastapol, CA: Nan Koehler, 1989.

Lang, Raven. *Blessingway into Birth*. Santa Cruz, CA: 1993.

Louden, Jennifer. *The Pregnant Woman's Comfort Book: A Self-Nurturing Guide to Your Emotional Well-Being During Pregnancy and Early Motherhood*. San Francisco: Harper Collins, 1995.

Marks, Kate. *A Circle of Song*. Amherst, MA: Full Circle Press, 1993.

McAnally, Mary. "Our Mother's Body is the Earth" in *Anthology of Magazine Verse and Yearbook of American Poetry*, ed. Alan F. Pater. Beverly Hills, CA: Monitor Book Company, 1980.

Montagu, Ashley. *Life Before Birth*. New York: New American Library, 1964.

Morgan, Robin. "Blessed Be" in *Lady of the Beasts: Poems by Robin Morgan*, New York: Random House, 1976.

Napierala, Susanna. *Water Birth: A Midwife's Perspective*. Westport, CT: Bergin & Garvey, 1994.

The New Farm Vegetarian Cookbook. Summertown, TN: Book Publishing Company, n.d.

Parker, Cindy. "The Blessingway." *Mother's Underground*. n.p. n.d.

—. *Ma Parker's Song Booklet*. n.p.: Healing Heart Herbals, 1995.

Parvati Baker, Jeannine. "Healing Cesarean Section Trauma: A Transformational Ritual" in *The Goddess Celebrates: An Anthology of Women's Rituals*, ed. Diane Stein,

210-216. Freedom, CA: Crossing Press, 1991.

Peterson, Gayle. *Birthing Normally: A Personal Growth Approach to Childbirth*. Oakland, CA: Bookpeople, 1984.

—. *An Easier Childbirth: A Mother's Guide for Birthing Normally*. Berkeley, CA: Shadow & Light, 1994.

Pinkola Estes, Clarissa. *Women Who Run With the Wolves*. New York: Ballantine Books, 1992.

Resnick Levine, Elizabeth. *A Ceremonies Sampler: New Rites, Celebrations, and Observances of Jewish Women*. San Diego: Women's Institute for Continuing Jewish Education, 1991.

Robins, Sue. "The Blessingway: An Alternative Baby Shower." *Canadian Women's Health Network Magazine*, 4, no. 1 (Winter 2001): 1.

Robinson, Janice. Pride & Joy: *African American Baby Celebrations: A Planning Guide for Baby Showers and Naming Ceremonies*. New York: Pocket Books, 2001.

Sale, Robin. "Creating a Blessing Way Ceremony." *The Doula* (Winter 1992): 12 - 14.

Scheerer Whitney, Laura. *Blessing the Way*. Ojai, CA: Sage Mountain Films, 1998. Videocassette Guidebook.

Spice, Becky. "Tibetan Bells." *BirthWorks National Newsletter of BirthWorks Childbirth Educators and Doulas* (Winter 2000).

Stein, Diane. *Casting the Circle: A Women's Book of Ritual*. Freedom, CA: Crossing Press, 1990.

Thompson, Lori. http://www.attachmentscatalog.com (accessed January 2002).

Tonder Hansen, Maren. *Mother-Mysteries*. Boston: Shambhala, 1997.

Walker, Barbara G. *Women's Rituals*. San Francisco: Harper and Row, 1990.

INDEX

A
Adoption 153
Altar 95
Appreciations 79
Arches 116

B
Baby Shower 1
Beads 90
Bells 54
Belly Masks 106
Birthdays 164
Blossoming 130
Bracelet, Blessingway 81

C
Candlelighting 83
Card Shower 139
Ceremonial Atmosphere 40
Ceremonial Progression 47
Ceremonies, Sample 143
Cesarean Section 161
Chanting 52
Chants and Songs,
    alphabetical listings 187
Circle of Love 121
Corner Stones 103
Cradling 120

D
Dancing 53
Diné 2
Diapers, embroidered 111
Divorce 168
Drumming 55

F
Fears 105
Feasts 131
Flowers 74

Footwashing 69

G
Gifts from the Heart 95
Grieving 157
Grooming 69

H
Hairbrushing 73
Hand Meditation, the 62
Hats, Crazy Ribbon 105
Headwreaths 74
Henna 77
Herbal bath 140

I
Invitations 27
Invocations 57

J
Journey, the (meditation) 65

L
Laying on of Hands 122
Libations 128
Long-Distance Blessingways
    138

M
Massage 123
Meal Trains 136
Meditations, Guided 62
Men 18
Menarche, onset of 164
Miscarriage 161
Moon Salutations 124

N
Naming 79
Navajo 2

Necklaces 90

P
Prayer Showers 115

Q
Quilts 110

R
Readings 86
RSVP's 40

S
Shirts 103, 111
Silence 61
Singing 52
Sisters Ceremonies 166
Smudging 60
Songs and Chants,
    alphabetical listings 187
Stillbirth 157
Storytelling 88

T
Tattoos 78
Toning 57
Tree-Planting 112
Trust walk 118

W
Walkabout 128
Wishes for Baby 101

Y
Yoga 124

ABOUT THE AUTHOR

Shari Maser is the home-educating mother of Alex and Erica. As a Certified Childbirth Educator (CCE), she has been facilitating BirthWorks classes and attending births in Ann Arbor, Michigan since 1999. Blessingways have played an influential role in her pregnancies and her parenting.

Give the Gift of
Blessingways

YES, please send _____ copies of *Blessingways: A Guide to Mother-Centered Baby Showers* at $14.95 each plus $5 shipping per book within the 50 United States or $10 shipping per book outside the USA. Michigan residents please add $0.90 sales tax per book.

My check or money order for $_____ is enclosed.

Please charge my: AMEX ❑   VISA ❑   MASTERCARD ❑   DISCOVER ❑

Name _____

Address _____

City _____ State ____ Zip _____

Phone (____)_____E-mail_____

Credit card number _____ Expiration (MM/YY)_____

Signature_____Date_____

Ship to (if different):

Name _____

Address _____

City _____ State ____ Zip _____

Please make your check payable and return to:
Moondance Press, Attn: Customer Service
4830 Dawson Drive, Ann Arbor MI 48103

Call your credit card order to: 734-426-1641

Fax your credit card order to: 732-446-6118

Place your online order at www.blessingway.net